HOW TO WRITE FOR THE
RELIGIOUS MARKETS

Also by BRENDA COURTIE

Not Quite Heaven
Jenny's Year
Glad Tidings for Groups (radio talks on audio cassette)
Christianity Explored (with Margaret Johnson)
Your Child and the Church

HOW TO WRITE FOR THE RELIGIOUS MARKETS

Brenda Courtie

ALLISON & BUSBY

First published in Great Britain in 1993 by
Allison & Busby
an imprint of Wilson & Day Ltd
5 The Lodge
Richmond Way
London W12 8LW

A catalogue record for this book is available from the British Library

ISBN 07490 0195 X

Typeset by TW Typesetting, Plymouth, Devon
Printed and bound in Great Britain by
Biddles Ltd, Guildford and King's Lynn

For my many Swanwick friends and tutors

CONTENTS

1

WRITING ABOUT RELIGION

Motives matter

So you want to write. Or more specifically, you want to write for the religious markets, which for the purposes of this book I take to be books, magazines and other 'word' products put together by and for the mainstream Christian sector. The principles are likely to be equally appropriate for those wishing to write for other religions, but the markets will of course be different.

Before you even start, the question has to be asked: 'Why? Why do you want to write? In particular, why do you want to write about religion?' Think hard, because your answer will determine whether or not you are likely to achieve any success with your writing.

Are you motivated more by your faith than by the desire to see yourself in print? You should be. Perhaps you feel that you have something to share which arises out of your personal religious experience and which you believe will be spiritually edifying for others, and you know that preaching is not the way for you. If your urge to communicate is allied to the appropriate writing skills (and we shall be looking at some of these later), then there is every chance of your work reaching that wider audience.

Are you compelled to write by something deep inside? Most successful writers write because they have to. This inner urge is not just some emotional kick-start, it is a very useful tractor that keeps you ploughing on in the face of rejection slips, demanding editors, fickle readers and changing markets. But don't worry if you only began to think about writing yesterday or suspect that you wouldn't miss it if you gave it up tomorrow. There is no divine rule that says you can only be published if you were born with the urge to write. (I say this from my own

1

experience.) If you know there is a market for something you believe you can write today, given the appropriate skills and the right guidance, then write it - but write it as well as you possibly can. If you're going to be remembered for just one piece, it had better be a good one.

Are you already good with words? As a speaker or preacher, perhaps? Or a raconteur? Or perhaps you enjoy writing long letters which the recipients re-read for themselves and then share with others? Communicating in print has its own rules and conventions, of course, but if you are prepared to become familiar with them then you could become a published writer.

Standards matter

'Ay, there's the rub', to quote one widely published writer. In religious writing, more than in any other writing sphere, there is a tendency to think that there is no need to learn the rules and apply the skills of commercial published writing.

The editors of religious magazines are constantly having to reject work submitted by such confidently insulated writers. One editor told me: 'They send me handwritten missives on bits of non-matching paper, often describing at inordinate length some dear soul's long illness, and finishing with the catch-all ending - it was only their wonderful faith that pulled them through. Or perhaps it is a long dissertation on the awful retribution awaiting anyone who does not agree with the writer about the great significance of some remote verse of scripture. There is often a covering letter informing me that the Lord has decreed that this particular piece is to be published. Which makes me wonder why the Lord has not said as much to me, and why He does not also decree that writers study the market before they put pen to paper!'

Behind the slightly exasperated humour, there are serious issues raised here which point up exactly where religious writing is different from secular writing. And - perhaps more importantly - where it is not.

Religious writing *is* different insofar as the writer believes that God can, and perhaps will, 'speak' through the printed words to the reader. But these printed words through which God may choose to speak are part of a hi-tech process for the dissemination of information which began with Gutenberg and which has been honed and polished into the world of publishing as we know it today.

Religious books and magazines are part of that world. They do not just drop out of the sky. They are published by responsible bodies who have to meet certain requirements, such as circulation targets and financial viability. They are compiled by editors who select material suited to the readers' interests and the publisher's editorial policy. They are written by people who have something to say which accords with the readers' interests and the publisher's policy, and who can say it in a thoroughly professional way.

An editor's desk is an editor's desk, whether the material landing on it from the postbag is about ecology or eschatology. If the manuscript is typed in the usual way – double spaced, with a good black ribbon, on A4 paper, one side only, pages numbered, right number of words, informative cover sheet on top – then the editor will be pleasantly disposed towards it. This manuscript looks professional, which gives a clue that the writer will have taken a similarly professional approach in taking the trouble to study the market and tailor the piece accordingly. (You will find detailed information about presentation and market study in Chapter 3.)

If, on the other hand, an envelope disgorges several sheets of semi-legible handwriting, the message the editor gets is that this manuscript comes from a rank amateur who has not even taken the trouble to have the piece typed, and therefore is unlikely to have made the effort to discover the publication's requirements. It would be a most charitable editor with time to spare who did not immediately mark it with a big 'no'.

A person who can sing in the bath would think very seriously before booking a concert hall and having tickets printed; at the very least, he would be well advised to take a few extra lessons and put in plenty of practice before going public. You may have enjoyed writing essays at school, or reports for the church magazine, but writing for a wider audience requires a new, professional standard. Some of the basic writing techniques you will need are dealt with in this book, but they are spelled out in much greater detail in other books in the same series which you will find listed on p. 149.

A writer who wants to share some spiritual insight with others cannot afford to ignore the normal expectations of the publishing world; neither can he ignore the normal expectations of the audience. If religious publications do not drop out of the sky, neither do their readers. They are ordinary people whose culture, education and language skills have conditioned them to warm to the kind of well-ordered and accessible writing they find in the best non-religious publications. So they will baulk at badly written irrelevancies from untrained communicators who seem to operate on the premise that professional skills are not required for anything religious.

Beliefs matter

There is a very positive spin-off for religious writers who have learned their craft. You can apply what you have learned to writing for the secular field. You can study a secular market and tailor your writing to fit it. But I must put in a warning here that this doesn't work the other way around. Writing for the religious markets is not just a matter of learning and applying the writing craft. To write Christian literature of whatever kind - articles, biographies, novels - you really do have to understand the Christian Gospel, the 'god spel' of rescue for humanity through Jesus the Son of God.

Commitment matters

Even if you are a committed believer, are well motivated and have mastered the skills, the very activity of writing is not as effortless as some people imagine. If you are one of those who think that writing of any kind is 'easy' compared with 'real work', I can only assume that you haven't tried it yet. Any successful writer - religious or secular - will tell you that writing is mentally and physically taxing in a way that those who don't do it cannot begin to appreciate. The battle to get the right words in the right order takes the kind of stamina which is as much a matter of healthy diet and regular sleep as mere perseverance. So please don't think about religious writing as some kind of convalescence or retreat. It's more like mountaineering - or worse, mountaineering on your own.

Writing is, of course, a solitary pursuit. For some people, this is its main attraction. You don't have to join a club (though there are many useful writers' organisations, some of which are listed in Chapter 15), and you don't have to be part of a firm (though if you're writing to be published, you are part of a team - again, see Chapter 15).

Perhaps you are drawn to writing because you enjoy - or at least can tolerate - being alone for hours at a time. But there are drawbacks to this kind of independence. Writing in a vacuum without any kind of sounding-board or encouragement can be very dispiriting, when you're not sure you're on the right track and you press on with the sinking feeling that all today's work may well have to be wiped off by the 'delete' button tomorrow. And if you don't actually live on your own, your nearest and dearest will have to understand that after battling away at your desk with your words, you may not have any words left for socialising. Writers can be very poor company after a session at the keyboard.

It goes without saying that you won't be writing for riches and glory. There are very few rich writers, even in the secular field, and I think probably none at all writing for the religious markets. Many of the 'famous names' that you would recognise on the shelves of a Christian bookshop have a 'proper' job apart from their writing - or at least a supportive spouse who has a 'proper' job. Some writers support themselves and their families by diversifying - writing for many different kinds of outlets and maybe doing some teaching or guest-speaking. So it is not impossible to make a living out of writing for religious markets, if you are prepared to take the downs along with the ups. But the ups are a mixed blessing - if your work is brilliant, some readers will praise God for it and some might also praise you for it, but in the religious field there will always be those who disagree with what you say or the way that you say it.

You may think I am being very gloomy about this religious writing business, but I am just trying to be realistic. After all, it was Jesus Himself who told the story of the man who set about building a tower without considering the cost of the project and then had to live with failure and humiliation. It is only fair that you should know the cost before you start. The purpose of this book is to help you meet that cost and do a job you won't be ashamed of.

Markets matter

So you still want to write? Fine. But now there is another question before we move on, and that is: 'Who are you writing for?'

Are you writing for yourself? There is a lot to be said for it. The therapeutic value of committing emotions and experiences to paper is well known, but it does pose a danger for people writing for the personal-experience markets (see Chapter 2) or religious-autobiography markets (see Chapter 4). In all religious writing, you are writing for yourself, in that you will naturally want to do the very best job possible for the sake of your own self-esteem; but that said, if you hope to be published, you are not writing merely for yourself, you are deliberately writing for an audience, writing to communicate.

Are you writing for God? Well, yes, if by that you mean that you are determined to honour God by writing as well as you possibly can. The young man who came to fit a gas fire at our house did a superbly neat job, and swept up so well that the room was cleaner when he'd finished than it had been when he started. When I pointed this out, he shrugged and said: 'I like to do a good job. I'm paid by the gas board, but I'm working for God.' But he was working for me too, and I liked what he did. Your reader should like what you do when you're writing for God.

Are you writing for the reader, or the publisher? In fact, there's no difference, because your work will only reach the reader after the publisher has read it and published it. This means that as a writer you need to be aware of both publishing policy and reader interest. In practice, you are writing for the reader, because the publisher will only commission work which his targeted reader is likely to buy. This is all part of your 'market study', which is dealt with more fully in Chapter 3.

Be assured, though, that there are readers out there waiting to read what you write. There are people in plenty who will buy religious books and magazines because they want to be encouraged by other people's religious experiences. They want to be informed about religious matters. They want to be stimulated in their own religious pursuits. But, as the preacher David Pawson was once told by an elderly pastor: 'It's not just getting it off your reel, but on to his bobbin!' If you are to help the reader on his own personal pilgrimage you have to communicate effectively.

The purpose of this book is to show you how to do just that.

2

WRITING YOUR RELIGIOUS INSIGHTS

Something to share?

Let us now go back to the question I posed at the beginning of this book: 'Why do you want to write?' We considered the matter of motivation in some detail because it is important, but for most religious writers the answer in a nutshell is usually: 'Because I have something to share.'

They have perhaps been blessed with a powerfully moving conversion experience, or it may just be that they have learned some small spiritual lesson which none the less became a significant turning point in their life, and now there comes the feeling that here is a story which is worth telling for the benefit of others.

Sharing experiences like this is not the preserve of religious writers. It is a universal human activity that goes back into prehistory. The hunter who returned to the cave and enthralled his hearers with tales of the chase engaged and entertained his audience in exactly the same way as today's secular story- writers and dramatists: by painting a vivid word-picture, the story-teller would arouse an empathetic response by evoking the same emotions in the audience that he had experienced during the hunt.

No doubt the hunter's tale often contained tips or warnings that other hunters could learn from. And it is here that we see the beginnings of the dynamics of much religious writing. When we feel we have something to share, it is because our experience has helped us and we believe that the recounting of it could also help others.

But is this 'shared-learning-through-recounted-experience' kind of writing always strictly religious? A quick glance at some of the popular women's weekly magazines will reveal that it is not. The 'genre' name for this kind of writing is 'inspirational writing' and of course there are markets for a good deal of inspirational writing which is not strictly religious (see Chapter 14).

However, the religious writer has a particular reason for wanting to share a learning experience with others. When we are motivated by the desire to help the reader to know more about God and His dealings with His people, then this kind of inspirational writing is properly called 'devotional writing'.

You have possibly already recounted your particular experience to a friend or a group of friends. It is because you believe your experience has a message for an even wider audience that you now consider writing it. Not many of us are called to the pulpit or the podium, so sharing our insights in print is an obvious alternative. And it has the added advantage of recreating the one-to-one dynamic of a friendly conversation where one party benefits from the experience of the other. Writing is the ideal medium if you have something personal that is worth sharing, rather than a forceful message that needs preaching.

But just as there are good preachers who know exactly how to win their audience and punch their message home (and bad ones who do not!), there are writers who know how to hit the mark with their readers. In devotional writing, you use the various ways and means of conveying effectively what you want to say, of recreating that personal encounter, so that the individual hears what you are saying and responds accordingly.

The 'shared-learning-through-recounted-experience' piece of devotional writing can be constructed in one of three ways, according to the complexity and significance of the experience and the appropriate length required to share it.

For convenience I shall call these three models:

- the *thought for the day* (200 words)
- the *lesson from life* (400 words)
- the *personal-experience article* (1,000-plus words).

This chapter shows how these three pieces are constructed, and includes some published examples.

Thought for the day

The *thought for the day* links a specific incident or idea from real life with a simple Bible teaching. The incident itself can be seemingly unimportant or insignificant, but it is something which made the writer think: 'That reminds me of . . .'. The writer then links the incident with some spiritual truth contained in the Bible. When you make this link, you are doing two things for your readers: you are showing how the real-life incident triggered a new or renewed understanding of God and His dealings with His people, and you are encouraging your readers to apply this same spiritual truth to their own situation.

When you write a *thought for the day* piece, you start by describing the real-life incident or idea. This can be taken either from your own experience or from some other source, such as an incident which happened to someone you know, or perhaps an incident which happened to a famous person the readers will know. Then you show how the incident or idea is a kind of analogy, a portrayal of some teaching point. You then go on to spell out how this lesson is applicable in every day and age, perhaps by directly urging readers to apply it in their own situations, or possibly by the more subtle method of stating how you, the writer, intend to apply the lesson in your own life in future. You would usually include a relevant Bible reference at the beginning or the end, or even at the point where you switch from the incident to the teaching.

Here is a *thought for the day* piece which appeared in a regional Mothers' Union magazine:

'Words, words, words!' We all remember Eliza Doolittle's exasperation with Freddie's declaration of love. 'Don't talk of love – show me!'

Actions might speak louder, but we can't really do without words. Indeed, for some people, words are the tools of their craft, to be used with care and precision. Ad-writers and novelists alike know the power of words, and also the power of a sub-text that can be concealed within and behind words. I gather it was Fay Weldon who gave us 'Go to work on an egg' and Salman Rushdie who conjured up 'Naughty but nice!' to sell cream cakes.

Christians need to be careful with words, simply because of this power they have to carry hidden messages. A Sunday gospel reading from the King James Bible which began: 'And Jesus took His disciples apart in the way' raised a few smiles from those of us who know what it's like to be taken apart by our superiors!

Words can be traitors. Sometimes you send them off with one message and they deliver a completely different message at the other end. Which is why I've recently given up talking about Jesus as 'Saviour' – Saviour needs explaining. But in a disaster-ridden world like ours, everyone knows what a 'Rescuer' is.

Col. 1.5: Of this you have heard in the word of truth.

The *thought for the day* is the kind of short piece you might find on the corner of a page in a religious newspaper, or even in your local weekly. Some editors like different contributors each time, while others prefer a series written by a regular contributor of almost columnist status, so it is wise to check before sending anything. There is no reason why you should not be the next regular contributor. Send a query letter asking if the editor would like to see the first six of a series.

Anthologies of these devotional daily thoughts are used by Christians and others all over the world. Again, some are collections from the writings of one person, but others are made up of thoughts from different contributors. *The Upper Room*, the world's most widely used devotional guide, is available from Methodist Publishing House, 20 Ivatt Way, Westwood, Peterborough, PE3 7PQ, and is always open to new contributors – but do study the booklet before submitting anything (see Chapter 3). Other *thought for the day* books and booklets are available from religious booksellers.

Individual *thought for the day* pieces are often used by national 'inset' magazines, which are stapled inside local church magazines (see Chapter 13).

Lesson from life

The *lesson from life* is similar to the *thought for the day* in that it links a real-life incident with a piece of Bible teaching. However, the *lesson from life* is longer, and the incident is nearly always taken from the writer's own experience. This allows you to give more detail and to explore more fully the feelings and emotions the incident aroused, which makes for better reader identification and empathy as the reader thinks: 'Oh, I've felt like that, too!'

As in the shorter piece, you start with a real-life incident, painting the necessary picture to show how the incident became a turning point or learning point for you. You tell the anecdote in such a way as to take the reader into the situation with you, so that the reader experiences the same sense of revelation as the penny drops and the lesson is learned. You can do this by conveying what you saw, heard and felt in an easy, almost conversational style.

After making the link to the Bible teaching with a suitable short quotation or reference, you round off the piece by referring back to the trigger incident, perhaps remarking that, whenever you find yourself in a similar situation again, you will be reminded of this teaching.

Here is a *lesson from life* which appeared in the church magazine 'inset' *Home Words*:

It's very peaceful in my kitchen at the moment, and I'm enjoying a quiet five minutes. But I can't sit for too long because I must set to on cleaning this floor. One of the kids spilled some orange squash and it's horribly sticky underfoot.

You know how it is. You're pottering about, clearing things away, making room for another pile of ironing, and suddenly the soles of your shoes turn to toffee.

I wasn't actually here when Number Two Son spilled his drink. I came in from the garden with some washing just after the event, and I assumed that the 'juice' he was dabbing at was the remains of a diluted glass of squash.

It was only later when I found myself tackying about like a duck that's been paddling in Evostick that I realised he'd in fact upset the bottle of concentrated stuff.

When he wandered back into the kitchen for yet another biscuit, I yelled at him: 'Why didn't you tell me you'd upset the squash bottle? I thought it was your drink on the floor. I sound like the school nurse ripping someone's sticking plaster off!'

'But I did tell you!' he protested. 'When I said I'm sorry I spilled the juice, I meant the stuff in the bottle. I dropped it trying to get the lid off. It was full.'

'Well it's not full now, is it?' I snorted. 'This floor's absolutely covered in concentrated orange.'

Number One Son had joined us by this time. 'Hardly surprising,' he quipped, 'as that's what it says on the label. Pity it wasn't floor cleaner.'

That was when I hit top doh, they fled, and I abandoned the laundry in favour of filling the kettle.

While I've been sipping my restorative coffee, I've also been thinking. Last week in a friend's house, I noticed the 'motto for the day' on her kitchen calendar. It said: 'Be filled with the spirit. What fills is what spills.' I suppose the reference was to the 'fruit of the Spirit' in Galatians 5.22 – love, joy, peace, patience, kindness, goodness, faithfulness, humility and self-control.

What fills is what spills. It's a sobering thought. One little knock, and look what spilled out of me, never mind the squash bottle! Temper, impatience, exaggeration, you name it.

A busy kitchen's not a bad place to learn the Christian life. What spills out when you get knocked?

You will find features like this in the 'inset' magazines mentioned above, and also in *Christian Family*, Elm House, 37 Elm Road, New Malden, Surrey, KT3 3HB. British contributions are encouraged in *Decision*, 1300 Harmon Place, Minneapolis, Minnesota, 55440-1988 and in many of the American magazines listed in *Writers' Market* (see Chapter 3).

Personal-experience article

Longer still than the *lesson from life* is the full-blown *personal-experience article*. And because it is even longer, you will need to know and use more tools of the writer's trade to ensure that your message gets across. The *personal-experience article*, while recounting a true story, makes full use of various fiction techniques, such as character development and dialogue. You can read about these and other fiction techniques in *Writing Step by Step* by Jean Saunders, *How to Write Stories for Magazines* by Donna Baker and *The Craft of Novel-Writing* by Dianne Doubtfire, all in the Allison & Busby *Writer's Guides* series. However, it is in its structural shape that the religious *personal-experience article* is closely linked with another popular genre.

Did you know that most of the personal experience stories in the popular true confession magazines are in fact pieces of fiction crafted by writers to read like real-life drama? These pieces come across as real and dramatic because of two basic techniques: (i) they are written in the first person (the writer tells of 'what happened to me'), and (ii) they are structured in a way that rivets the reader's attention from the start and keeps them reading to the end.

The story opens either with a significant incident which foreshadows a point of change in the writer's life, or at the actual point of high drama. There must be a reader-hooking opening sentence. Having grabbed the reader's attention, posing all kinds of unwritten and unanswered questions - 'Who is this? Why are they in this situation? What are they going to do about it? - you then use 'flashback' to take the reader back in time to when events leading up to the drama began gradually to unfold. ('Flashback' is dealt with in Donna Baker's *How to Write Stories for Magazines*, mentioned above.)

The story usually consists of up to twelve scenes, not arranged in chronological order, but starting either with a significant incident or the actual crisis at the heart of the story, then filling in the build-up to that turning point via the earlier scenes. When you reach your starting scene, you move on to what happened next until you reach the story's end.

If you decide to start at a point of high drama, when you get back there again, that will serve as a kind of pivot. It is the point where you, the writer and main character, begin to realise new truths and make decisions which will change the course of your life from here on.

If you decide to start at a related significant incident, and save the drama so that it has more impact in the story's development, then your starting scene will not be the pivot - that comes with the drama.

The diagrams illustrate how flashback can be used in the personal experience article:

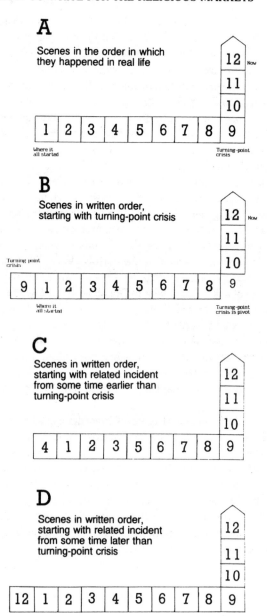

A

Scenes in the order in which they happened in real life

| 1 | 2 | 3 | 4 | 5 | 6 | 7 | 8 | 9 |

12 Now
11
10

Where it all started

Turning-point crisis

B

Scenes in written order, starting with turning-point crisis

Turning point crisis

| 9 | 1 | 2 | 3 | 4 | 5 | 6 | 7 | 8 | 9 |

12 Now
11
10

Where it all started

Turning-point crisis is pivot

C

Scenes in written order, starting with related incident from some time earlier than turning-point crisis

| 4 | 1 | 2 | 3 | 5 | 6 | 7 | 8 | 9 |

12
11
10

D

Scenes in written order, starting with related incident from some time later than turning-point crisis

| 12 | 1 | 2 | 3 | 4 | 5 | 6 | 7 | 8 | 9 |

12
11
10

14

Like the shorter devotional pieces already mentioned, the *personal-experience article* presents the reader with a lesson based on a real-life incident throwing new light on a Bible teaching.

The scenes that come after the climax tell the reader what happened as a result of the lessons learned and how everything was finally resolved. Using the techniques of fiction, the skilled writer will have portrayed the main character and the central situation so well that the reader is left wondering: 'What did they do after it was all over? Where are they now?' But there will be the abiding conviction that the character was made a stronger/kinder/better person because of their response to the traumatic events told in the story. And the unstated but very clear message is that there is similar light at the end of the tunnel for readers in their own difficulties.

Here is an extract from a *personal-experience article* which appeared in *Decision* magazine. The article begins with the writer at the word processor thinking about 'explaining the gospel' and how it was first explained to her by a college friend. Then there's a flashback to the time when the writer was an insecure and unhappy student whose attempt to run away from college had been foiled by a caring tutor who intercepted her at the railway station. This is the crisis which becomes a turning point in the writer's life:

In silence we drove back to college, but I wept tears of frustration at my double failure; I couldn't even succeed in running away.

My fellow students were still in lectures when I crept back into my shared college bedroom. I sat on my bed and wondered whether I could grit my teeth and persevere. I doubted it. But there seemed no other option.

'I hate this place,' I said out loud, and I'd probably have flung myself weeping into my pillow if there hadn't been a knock at the door.

'Can I come in?'

It was Jacquie, second clarinettist in the college orchestra; she was already in the room, so I nodded. Jacquie lived across the landing and we saw enough of each other in music classes for me to think of her as a friend.

It occurred to me that Jacquie might be just the person to provide me with a few clues for survival. She too was a church-goer.

'Jacquie,' I said, 'doesn't it bother you, all this business about "There's no such thing as God" and "Every man is his own moral governor?" I mean, you believe in God, don't you?'

'I should hope so!' she laughed.

'But how is it these liberal ideas don't rattle you as they do me?'

'The thing is, Brenda,' she replied, 'they can say there's no God, but I have a day-by-day relationship with Him. To them, He's a topic for debate. To me, He's a real and powerful Person. So I don't have to prove God's existence to myself by scoring points off the others. Do you follow?'

I hadn't realised that Jacquie's quiet unruffled approach to life was not just one of those 'personality traits' I'd been learning about in psychology. Suddenly I felt a flutter of hope stir inside me. If it weren't just a matter of personalities, maybe I could get to where Jacquie was.

The writer goes on to describe how Jacquie explained the gospel to her in a way that changed her outlook and gave her the assurance and confidence she had lacked before. There's a summary of the writer's adult life, married to a partner who shares her commitment to explaining the gospel to others. The piece finishes with the writer at the word processor as at the beginning, composing a leaflet to 'explain the gospel' to the local church house groups.

Many magazines and papers will take well-written personal-experience stories. For example, they have appeared in *Christian Family* (address above); *Woman Alive*, Herald House Publications, 96 Dominion Road, Worthing, West Sussex, BN14 8JP; *Christian Herald* (same address); *Decision* (address above - they particularly like personal-experience articles describing conversion to Christ); *Challenge*, Revenue Buildings, Chapel Road, Worthing, West Sussex, BN11 1BQ.

In addition to religious outlets, there are markets for the inspirational *personal-experience article* in the secular press, which is dealt with in Chapter 14.

So - have *you* got something to share? Whether your special insight lends itself to the *thought for the day* slot, the *lesson from life* slot or the *personal-experience article* slot, your devotional writing will reveal some aspect of truth for the reader. How effectively that truth is revealed depends in the end on how well you write your piece.

Good devotional writing is sincere and written from conviction but it calls for honesty and humility. It uses careful detail to show how ordinary events can portray spiritual truths. And it is both generous and gentle. Yes, you present your special insights and the resulting options, but you leave the reader to draw any necessary conclusions and make any appropriate applications for themselves. Remember, you are recreating the one-to-one dynamic of a friendly conversation, not preaching hell-fire!

3

WRITING FOR A MARKET

Who is it for?

When you are sure you want to write for the right reasons, and you have some idea of what you want to write about, the obvious next step is to decide who you will be writing for. Notice the future tense - I use it quite deliberately! Many would-be writers scribble or tap away at their masterpiece until it is in a state that pleases them (and it has to be said that too often this is no more than a breathless but not faultless first draft), and then they start looking around for somewhere to send it.

If you are new to writing, this may indeed seem like the obvious and logical way of going about things. But to quote John Hines, successful writer and writing tutor, this method is 'about as logical as a dentist making dentures and then looking for a patient they might fit'. Writers who write first and then start hawking their product around the editors and publishers are almost certain to encounter a lot of unnecessary frustration and bewilderment in the face of repeated rejection, especially if the rejected writing is good and genuinely of interest.

Experienced writers do not start the actual writing - apart from notes, ideas, plans and drafts - until they have thoroughly researched the market and carefully selected the most appropriate magazine or publisher for the kind of writing they want to do. Then, and only then, can they begin to put together a written piece that is absolutely tailor-made for the selected outlet.

Now this is no cast-iron guarantee against rejection, but it does ensure that an editor will not brush your work aside with such comments as: 'We never use articles this long/short' or 'This subject is totally against our denomination's beliefs' or 'We've already done a piece/book just like this.'

One of the hardest lessons you have to learn as a writer is that no editor or publisher is going to change the whole shape of his magazine or publishing list in order to accommodate your brilliant writing if your piece does not fit his requirements. I have watched students in my writing classes struggle against this fact, sending off beautifully written pieces all over the place with little or no success. I have also seen the same students begin selling their work consistently once they started tailoring their writing to specifically targeted markets. You really do have to *study the market*, *target a slot* and *tailor your piece* to fit it.

Writing for the reader

All magazine editors and book publishers have a very clear policy concerning their product and its contents. They know exactly who their potential readers are and they also know what are the interests, aspirations and expectations of these readers. And, just as importantly, they know exactly the kind of writing that will attract them – the most appropriate subject, writing style and length.

Of course, the readers have to be satisfied or they won't buy the book or magazine. But there are other considerations which also govern an editor's or publisher's requirements. For example, in secular magazine publishing, the advertisers have to be satisfied that the magazine will attract the sort of readers who might be persuaded to buy the advertised products. It is the income from the advertisers which pays for the production and distribution of the magazine. Therefore the editor has to be sure that the pieces he buys from writers will keep attracting readers likely to buy the advertised goods.

Religious magazines may not be so dependent on advertising revenue in this way, but the same principles apply. Religious editors use pieces which satisfy targeted readers. In religious magazines, readers are targeted according to their religious persuasion, denomination, status in the church, age or whatever.

Reader-targeting for books is not linked to advertisers' preferences, of course. But religious publishers still have a targeted readership in view when it comes to subject, style and length. Targeted readers will be sympathetic to the theological stance of the publishing house. They will also be numerous enough to make the proposed book viable. All magazine editors and book publishers have therefore come up with their own particular pattern which they reckon will attract their targeted readership. They are looking for writers whose work fits their particular pattern.

Studying the market

So how do you know what this pattern is? You *study the market*. That is to say, you familiarise yourself with the *current* output from as many magazine or book publishers as possible. This way, you will be able to identify those magazines or books which already seem to present the kind of subject you might write about, in a style that is similar to your own, aimed at a readership that you too could 'speak to'.

Very often, these will be the books and magazines that you – the writer – already enjoy reading as a reader. So your first recourse in finding an appropriate outlet for your own writing might well be to ask yourself what books and magazines you enjoy reading yourself, and to start by checking the current output from those publishers.

The best way to examine the 'current output' of religious books is by browsing through the shelves of the largest Christian bookshop you can reach. This is one instance where I would advise you to ignore your local library, because while it will certainly have a religious section, the books will probably not be typical of what the publishers are doing right now.

Although Christian bookshop managers are extremely helpful and will usually answer customers' questions about market trends, many of the smaller bookshops are staffed by teams of part-time volunteers who may not have the same overview of the market or even of their own stock. So, in addition to browsing among the shelves, I would also suggest that you beg recent back-copies of the Christian booksellers' trade journals, which are chock-full of news about religious publishers and recent publications. You might even think it worthwhile subscribing to one of these journals yourself. They are the *European Christian Bookstore Journal*, Grampian House, 144 Deansgate, Manchester, M3 3EE, and *The Christian Bookseller*, 2 Forge House, Summerleys Road, Princes Risborough, Bucks, HP27 9DT.

Another way to get information about recent publications is from the publishers' catalogues which they will send you if you write and ask for them. You will find religious book and magazine publishers listed in the *Writers' and Artists' Yearbook* published by A&C Black, *The Writer's Handbook* published by Macmillan and *The Master List*, a Christian resources guide published by Capstone. Some religious magazines are also included in Gordon Wells's *The Magazine Writer's Handbook* (listed at the beginning of this book), which is also a good way to begin exploring the many secular magazines that religious writers could be writing for (see Chapter 14). These handbooks give not just the publishers' addresses, but also a brief summary of their usual requirements. Make sure you consult an up-to-date edition. There are also some market guides which are in magazine form and published monthly or quarterly with up-to-date news of publishers' and editors' requirements. For example, you will find *Freelance Market News* and *Freelance Writing and Photography* listed in the *Writers' and Artists' Yearbook* and *The Writer's Handbook*, and there is a useful bi-monthly called *Writers' Guide* available from G. Carroll, 11 Shirley Street, Hove, East Sussex, BN3 3WJ.

The larger Christian bookshops stock a wide range of religious magazines, but you can write direct for samples of others. For addresses, use the handbooks mentioned above. The 'magazines, journals and newspapers' section of *The Master List* is very useful here.

It is a good idea to try to picture in your mind – or even commit to paper – the 'typical reader' who is being targeted by a magazine. This is an easy task with the secular magazines. A careful study of the advertisements will reveal the kind of person being targeted – male or female, age-range, income group, their interests and whether they are home-based or career-based.

You can't get such a precise socio-economic profile from the religious magazines because the advertisers' criteria are different. But you can still work out whether the typical reader is likely to be young or more mature, evangelical, charismatic, academic, family-orientated, or whatever.

This 'picture the reader' exercise is actually great fun, and can become quite compulsive when you find yourself confronting a pile of magazines in a waiting room! But it is a vital exercise if you are hoping to write for a particular magazine, because you are going to have to write in a way that will be pleasing to that same targeted reader.

Targeting a slot

When you have pictured your reader by studying the advertisements, you then turn to the editorial content of the magazine. In terms of their written contents, most magazines are a mixed bag - a mixture of long and short pieces, a mixture perhaps of non-fiction (articles) and fiction (stories), and possibly also a mixture of serious and light topics. This mixed bag of various items has been gathered together to attract the targeted readers. But, whatever the mix, the regular reader likes to find the same kind of piece in roughly the same place in the magazine week by week or month by month. The editor has therefore decided what is the best order for these pieces, the best style and the best length, so that the magazine will have the necessary familiarity and also the right balance and freshness.

If you compare the actual 'Contents' list over several issues of a magazine, you will be able to tell which regular features are always written by the same person. In the secular magazines, these are the sections written by staff writers. In the religious magazines, there are often regular slots written by well-known church leaders or teachers. Obviously, it would be a complete waste of time trying to write something for these pages. However, there will be plenty of scope for the 'freelance' writer on the other pages.

As you become familiar with a particular magazine, you will find a 'slot' which seems to be appropriate for the piece you are thinking of writing. (If you don't, you need to study further magazines until you do.) Make sure that it *is* the right slot for you by checking several consecutive issues of the magazine until you really get the 'feel' of that particular section.

At this stage, you are in a position to analyse exactly what the editor likes to have in that slot week by week or month by month. What kind of piece is it, fiction or non-fiction? Personal experience? Interview? Biography? Bible exposition? Opinion? Self-help? How-to? et cetera. Is the 'tone' of the slot usually heavy, or is it light? What length is it?

At which point incredulous new writers ask, 'Do you mean I have to count the words?' The answer is yes, you do. Because if it is an 800-word slot and you send 600 or 1,000, the editor will probably not even read your piece. Counting printed words in magazines is easy. You take a ruler and count how many words there are in one inch (or 100mm) of a column of text in the middle of the piece. Then you measure the total length of all the columns and multiply. You do not have to be nit-pickingly precise – editors work to the nearest round fifty. Counting the words of your own piece of writing need be no more difficult. Your word-processor may do it for you, either in the corner of the screen as you work, or as a separate procedure, or as part of a spell-check. If you use a conventional typewriter, count a typical page and multiply. If you prefer to begin in longhand, always use the same kind of lined paper, count a typical page and make a note of it for regular rule-of-thumb reference before you type.

Books are also measured in numbers of words, to the nearest thousand. By choosing a larger or smaller typeface, a publisher can 'stretch' or 'squeeze' a manuscript to fit the appropriate number of pages, but as a general guide, an average adult fiction book would be 70,000 words. Many religious paperbacks are much shorter than that. This book *How to write for the Religious Markets* is 45,000 words.

Tailoring your piece

Now that you are thoroughly familiar with the slot you are aiming to fill, you can go ahead and write your piece. Naturally, it will be your piece. That is to say, you will not slavishly copy the work of a writer already published in that slot. But your piece will certainly win the editor's attention if it immediately seems to be the kind of thing that usually goes in that slot. So choose a topic that would sit well in that slot, and write in a way that 'speaks' with the right kind of tone for that slot. And make it not just the right length overall, but make your paragraphs and even your sentences the right length too.

You will find further help with particular kinds of writing in the appropriate chapters of this book.

Pleasing the editor

It may be unjust, but it is a fact that an editor is better disposed to expect something worthwhile from a manuscript that looks professional than from one that does not. So it is in every writer's best interests to make the submitted manuscript look absolutely perfect. Other books in this series give detailed guidance on how to put together a professional-looking manuscript, notably *The Craft of Writing Articles* by Gordon Wells and *The Craft of Novel-Writing* by Dianne Doubtfire. Here is my own list of 'ten tips for scrupulous scripts':

i) Your manuscript *must* be typed. Busy editors just don't have time to decipher your handwriting.

ii) Use plain white A4 paper, not the old quarto. (American editors often specify 8 in×11 in, but will accept submissions on A4 from UK contributors.) Type on one side only. Use a typewriter with a good black ribbon, or a word processor with a letter-quality printer.

iii) The main text of your writing ('copy') must be double-spaced and justified on the left only, not on the right. Leave a 40mm margin on the left of each page and a 25mm margin on the right, at the top and at the bottom. Indent paragraphs three spaces, but don't leave extra line-spaces between them. Leave only one space after a full-stop.

iv) Make your first page a 'cover sheet'. Name and address in top right-hand corner, title of your piece 120mm down the page in the centre (in capitals if you wish) but don't underline your title because underlining – to a printer – means you want something in italics when it is published. Under the title type 'by' in the centre, and under this type the name you wish to appear with the piece ('byline'). You can use a pseudonym here, but the cheque will be sent to the name with the address at the top of the cover sheet.

Leave several lines, then type on the left the approximate number of words in your piece – to the nearest 50 for articles and short stories, the nearest 1,000 for a book.

If you are submitting to a magazine or newspaper, a few lines below the number of words you should type FBSR. This stands for 'First British Serial Rights', which is what you are offering to the editor – the right to publish your piece for the first time in a publication which is issued periodically, i.e. in a 'series', hence 'serial'.

v) On your first page proper, leave an 80mm margin at the top, then type the title and byline as on the cover sheet. Begin your 'copy' a double-space below your byline, without indenting this first paragraph.

vi) At the top of the second page and all subsequent pages, type a key word from the title followed by the page number in numerals. At the bottom right of all pages except the last, type 'mf' to indicate that 'more follows'. On the last page, type 'End' in the centre below the last line of your copy. Type your name and address in the bottom right-hand corner of the last page, single-spaced. For a book, keep numbering consecutively throughout – don't start new numbers for each chapter.

vii) Make copies of all your pages to keep while you send out the orginal typescript.

viii) Short pieces should be fastened with a paperclip at the top left-hand corner. Complete book manuscripts should be packed without fastenings in an A4 box such as those containing A4 paper that you buy, but in the first instance, send a book publisher only a synopsis of the whole work, plus a proposal if it's a non-fiction book or two chapters if it's a novel.

ix) Use a C4 (324mm×229mm=13in×9in) envelope for sending short pieces. Enclose a brief letter and a stamped addressed envelope for the possible return of your manuscript, or stamps in the case of a complete book manuscript.

x) When submitting poetry, type each poem on a separate sheet and put your name and address on every sheet.

Committed Christians who are new to writing for the religious markets sometimes question this business of studying the market and producing a perfect typescript of a tailored piece for a targeted slot. It all sounds rather 'worldly' if you believe God has given you something to say. If it is from God, the argument goes, surely the editor will print it no matter what form it comes in? We have already seen why he won't in Chapter 1, but here I would add that there is no scriptural mandate for shoddiness in God's kingdom – rather the opposite – and anyway, what's wrong with learning a new skill to use for the extending of that kingdom?

4

WRITING YOUR AUTOBIOGRAPHY

Not just for the famous

If you have read Chapter 2 of this book, which deals with the personal experience article, you may have been thinking, 'Yes, but so many things in my life are worth sharing.' Or maybe your particular personal experience was so significant that a short article would not do it justice? In either case, you may well be thinking of writing a book.

Judging by the number of unsolicited life-stories that land in my in-tray for comment, it would seem that ninety per cent of all church people are currently writing a book, the *same* book, in that they all seem to be writing their autobiography. Which is fair enough, because I do believe the saying is true that we *all* have a book inside us – the story of our own pilgrimage thus far.

However, it is also true that general publishers are usually interested in an autobiography only if the writer is extremely famous or if their life has been so amazingly different and fascinating as to make the story absolutely unique and original. Stories from these people do not even have to be well written; the publisher's editor will make them readable, or a ghost-writer may even be commissioned to work the material into an absorbing book (see Chapter 12). But what chances are there for a not-terribly-well-known freelance religious writer wanting to write up his or her not-terribly-amazing life story?

Surprisingly, the chances are really quite favourable if you are writing for the UK religious market. (The same is not true in the US – see Chapter 14.) Just look at the autobiography section in any UK Christian bookshop. Some are indeed by famous people. Others are by people who tell of outstanding experiences – for example, remarkable conversion testimonies, or accounts of unexpected healing miracles. But many of the titles are by people who have told the story of their own pilgrimage in such a way that the simplest incidents reveal something of God's involvement with ordinary folk. Such stories inspire renewed faith on the part of the reader, so of course the religious publishers are fully aware of the potential readership for this kind of autobiography.

But a note of warning here. Writing a publishable autobiography takes more than the desire to recall and record one's memories, and of course there are extra and particular criteria for autobiographies aimed at the religious market.

Is it genuine?

Forgive me for being blunt, but some writers are so anxious to be positive and faith-building that they fall victim to the temptation to overstate the positive and forget about the negative. Interestingly, the Bible never does this. We marvel at the great achievements of God's people partly because we see them in all their mortality - warts and all - yet still being used and blessed by God.

If in recounting the wonders and miracles, or even just the glimpses of hope and the answered prayers, you leave out the disappointments and failures, your readers' initial elation will turn to disillusionment when God does not seem to work in the same way in their situation. Far from revealing the truth about the nature of God, you will have presented a limited and untrue picture of the way God works.

Is it original?

While it is a delight for readers to 'rejoice with those who rejoice and weep with those who weep', this is true only up to a point. I recently asked a Christian bookseller what he hoped *not* to see in the next batch of new releases. He said: 'Yet another testimony from a Christian healed from, or enduring, long-term illness, or from the parent of a child who has died.' Why? There are so many of these already, and while it is wonderful to know that God is doing great things in the lives of people in these circumstances, the reading public needs to know that He can do great things in *other* circumstances, too.

If, as you read this, your own story is being demolished before your very eyes, take heart. It's a matter of finding a new angle, an original slant, rather than just focusing on the perceived 'main event'. Publishers sometimes reject a testimony story because they feel it has been written up too close to the event. Perhaps, in retrospect, you can see the wider implications of what God was doing in terms of other members of the family or the church or the local community.

Even if you are not writing a 'signs and wonders' testimony, publishers will look for an original angle. Where are you now on your pilgrimage in relation to where you started out? Is there a particularly interesting reason for the route you followed? What changes to yourself, your circumstances, your family, friends or fellowship have come about because of the route you took?

What is your theme?

What we have been talking about here is the underlying *theme* of your autobiography. In a nutshell, what is your message? Of course, it can be said that all Christian autobiographies have the same overall theme: 'God is alive and well and active in my area.' But in order to identify with your experience and look to God to be active in their area too, your readers will be listening for the underlying theme specific to your book. This might be 'God still heals today', 'When you trust in God disasters lead to blessings', 'Faith in God helps you to endure intense suffering with patience and joy', 'God can change people beyond all recognition', 'God can mend a broken marriage', 'God's plans are bigger and better than our plans' and so on.

If you are to write an autobiography that is to be a blessing to your readers, it is important to identify your theme before you start your writing. I say this because your theme will dictate what you put in and what you leave out.

How do you structure your story?

Not all autobiographies tell the author's whole life-story. Even those which do are structured in such a way as to highlight those features which are relevant to the message, the underlying theme. These writers will barely touch on events less relevant to the forward movement and message of the book. A house-move may be an important turning point in one person's story, but not worth a mention in someone else's. On the other hand, something as seemingly trivial as changing the time of the morning alarm-call might mark the start of a new and significant development. Only you can decide what is relevant to the integrity of your story, because it is you, the writer, who have already decided what your story's message is to be.

If you are tackling your own life-story in its entirety to date, you will need to do as much editing as actual writing. This was my experience when I wrote my autobiography *Not Quite Heaven* (Triangle/SPCK 1984). I decided in advance which incidents I thought were necessary to make an interesting and coherent account *and* portray the theme; then, after writing the first draft, I removed some 'cul-de-sac' material and added new sections which helped the flow of the story. Some of these were forgotten memories which only came to the surface once I was writing, so I could not have considered them in advance, anyway.

Some autobiographies are limited to a particularly interesting or dramatic period in the writer's life. This allows scope for more detail and reflection, but without the natural forward movement of the fleeting years it is important to keep the pace moving and the pages turning. Two 'motors' which can keep the reader asking 'What happened next?' in a short time-span story are humour and tension. Humour makes them turn the pages in anticipation of another laugh; tension makes them turn the pages to discover the solution to the current dilemma.

A question that is often asked about structuring autobiography is: 'Should I make it chronological (beginning at birth or the start of the crisis), or use flashback (using the *personal-experience article* structure outlined in Chapter 2)?' Both forms have been well used, and both have been criticised as boring or clichéd. My feeling is that if the quality of the writing is good enough, then either form is acceptable. Another way in to your story is via an episode featuring a person who is significant to the whole book, or perhaps a place which has the same relevance, or indeed anything of significance which can be used as a unifying thread.

Make it interesting

You may think that the true facts as you recall them are what will make your story interesting to others, but this is not necessarily so. I once spent a week in the public gallery of a Crown Court - researching for a play - and discovered that a police report of the facts about a case can be the most boring and tedious part of the whole proceedings. Your reader does not want a report containing all the facts, but a grandstand view of the action, a front-row seat for the drama, an armchair in front of the screen for the picture. The best stories - fact or fiction - are those where you feel you are right there as it is all happening. And if you want to write a 'couldn't-put-it-down' autobiography, you will need to use more than the facts. You will need *feelings* and *fiction techniques*.

Feelings

You will be writing about yourself as a person, a human being with the same human feelings and emotional responses as your reader. Alongside the facts, weave in the feelings you experienced in the various situations, and indicate whether there were difficulties arising out of those feelings and how you coped with them. This not only portrays more of the truth in your 'true' story, it also builds a bond between you and your readers, as they (being as human as you) identify with your emotional responses.

Truth or fiction?

Writing about your feelings adds to the truth of your account, yes. But is there not a danger that using fiction techniques is in some way being less than truthful? I think that depends on what you mean by truth. To portray a real-life situation in which God has in some way intervened, and to portray it in a way which will build up the reader in their own faith, you have to make that real-life situation seem as real to them as it was to you.

You need to write about people who seem real, who speak, who have feelings, who react. You need to write about places which seem real, which have details that make a believable picture in the reader's imagination. The real truth is not a matter of whether someone had blond hair or used a particular turn of phrase; neither is it a matter of whether a table was oak or mahogany. The real truth is the message contained in your theme, the truth about the nature of God and His dealings with His people, which your reader discovers as he or she 'sees' real people in real situations discovering the same truth. And the way you make the reader 'see' like this is by using fiction techniques.

Fiction techniques

Let me give you an example. Here is a factual account of something that happened to me when I was a young music student:

> When I was a student, I was persuaded to join the college Trad Jazz Band, although I had no experience of this kind of music. However, they needed a tuba-player and as that was my instrument I went along to one of their rehearsals. The band consisted of Mike Edwards on trumpet, Paul Thompson on clarinet, Idris Price on trombone and Jim Clifton on piano. At that stage, the band did not have a drummer. At first I was very nervous, having only played classical music on tuba, like my book of *Twelve Russian Studies*, but everyone was very friendly, and I soon realised that Traditional Jazz consists of a lot of instinctive 'busking', such as I had seen my aunt doing on the piano when I was small.

As it stands, that is no more than a list of facts about the situation, the people and the outcome. Even my nervousness is listed as a fact.

Here is the same incident written up with the use of fiction techniques

to help the reader to 'see' real people developing and moving forward
in a real situation:

Encouraged by Mr Bradshaw, the brass tutor, who decided early on
that I had the makings of a fair tuba-player, I spent a lot of my time
'below stairs'. Relaxing in the peculiar solitude of a solo instrument
trapped by sound-proofed walls, I worked at my *Twelve Russian
Studies*, until they came to an abrupt halt one evening when the door
burst open and my sanctuary was invaded by two bearded young
men.

'There! I told you there was another one!'

'But she's a girl!'

'Of course she's a girl! What difference does it make? Is that or
is that not a tuba?'

'Right. That is certainly a tuba!'

It was a tuba of sorts. I'd handed back the youth orchestra
instrument to Mr Jenkins and was now learning on a college
instrument that had seen better days. It was badly dented, the leaky
water-key was fastened shut with knotted red string, and three of the
metal stays had come adrift and had been somewhat inadequately
reinforced with sticky tape.

'I'm sorry,' I said, 'is there some bother about me having this?
Mr Bradshaw said I could use it as my own.'

'And you're more than welcome, I should say!'

I'd already pinned him as a Welshman before his colleague
announced: 'Idris has his own wotsit, er, tuba. Trouble is, we need
him to play trombone in the band.'

I hadn't seen either of these characters in the college wind band,
that loud and lively siding where I'd been shunted along with all
the other brass and wind players not good enough for the college
orchestra.

So I asked, 'What band?'

'Why, the Jazz Band, of course!' said the Welshman. Only, the
way he said it, it sounded like Jass Band. Very authentic. Early New
Orleans.

'Can you play Dixieland on that thing?' demanded his friend.

'I don't know,' I answered with patent honesty. 'How does it go?'

When they'd finished laughing, the Welshman looked at the first of the *Twelve Russian Studies* and exclaimed, 'Hell, Mike! If she can get round this lot in three weeks, she won't have any trouble with "Tin Roof Blues".'

'Right, then,' said Mike, 'you're in!'

'In what?'

They answered in chorus. 'The Jazz Band!'

'But I've never played jazz!' I protested.

'That's what they all say!' laughed Mike.

As they left, Idris said: 'It's a giggle, love, honest. Large practice-room, piano block, eight o'clock tomorrow night. Tata!'

It is absolutely impossible to slip unnoticed into a room whilst carrying a battered old tuba that has a propensity for dropping bits with the capriciousness of a rattle- throwing baby. My entrance was greeted with loud cheers from the rest of the band, and Idris quickly did the introductions.

'Jim Clifton on piano, Drama and English. Paul, er, Thompson wasn't it. Yes, Paul Thompson on clarinet. He's a first-year musician like yourself.' I recognised the first clarinettist from the wind band.

'Mike Edwards on trumpet you've already met, English and Art. I'm going on to trombone now you're here, but I'm really the college's other tuba-player, Idris Price. Gentlemen, this is, er, Brenda. Right?'

'Right. I hope you told them I'm new to all this?'

'The way we play, love, you could do your Russian Studies and no one would notice!'

Jim stubbed out a cigarette in the ash-tray on top of the piano. 'Still no drums, Idris?'

'There's a first-year potter who's keen, but he can't count. I felt we had to draw the line of incompetence slightly above that!'

'Right then. Let's see how we do with "Darktown Strutters' Ball" for starters.'

When Jim swung into a tinkling intro with heavy bass, a thousand memories flooded back, of family 'do's' with Aunty Kath at the piano. Then as I watched the others blend into the first chorus together, another familiarity asserted itself. I'd done this before, surely? With Marj? Yes, of course! They were busking!

Oh, they paid allegiance to a common chord progression, a

'reference' melody and Jim's authoritative left hand. But within this framework they improvised freely.

I crept in on the second chorus, and found my way through the sequence as quietly as possible. For the third and final chorus, I opened up and 'oompahed' briskly round the appropriate bass-scales with some exhilaration.

After the 'Hi-tiddly-eye-tye, brown bread!' ending, they swooped on me.

'I thought you said you couldn't play?'

'Where did you learn to do that?'

'That was no Russian Study, now. Be honest!'

It's a truism in the music world that the professionals are the professionals because they play for their living. Meaning that if you can afford to spend all your time playing your musical instrument, you're bound to get good!

The improvement in my general tuba-playing during my time at Bretton Hall was in part due to the fact that I spent many hours playing it. And much of that time was with the Jazz Band. Traditional jazz became a hobby that paid dividends in agility and stamina for the Russian Studies and their like.

(From *Not Quite Heaven*, Brenda Courtie, Triangle/SPCK, 1984)

This time, the names - Mike Edwards, Paul Thompson, Idris Price and Jim Clifton - are not just names, but people who speak and act and react. My instrument - the tuba - is not described in terms of size and length of brass tubing, but is pictured as something that 'oompahs' on bass scales and has bits that tend to drop off. The lack of a drummer is conveyed in a humorous exchange between Jim and Idris. My feelings - nervousness giving way to confidence - are woven into the action through the use of words and phrases like *solitude, sanctuary, sorry, shunted, not good enough, patent honesty, impossible to slip unnoticed, I hope you told them, memories flooded back, another familiarity asserted itself, I crept in, opened up, with some exhilaration, a hobby that paid dividends.*

Fiction writers 'show' events happening rather than 'tell' about them in reported account. They make their characters speak in true-to-life dialogue. They reveal their characters' personalities through their speech and their actions. They convey mood or emotion through apt words of description threaded into the text. And all of these techniques can be used to advantage to make your autobiography a really good read.

Hindsight, boredom and jargon

The fiction techniques extract is from my 'pilgrimage' story, a religious autobiography published by a religious publisher, yet in this passage there is no mention of God or of my need for Him. Indeed, there is even a swear-word. That is because I wanted to portray God intervening in the life of a real, fairly insecure music student surrounded by a lot of real people who were both attractive and threatening. If I had used Christian hindsight and written of myself as a seeker in need of God or of my friends as unbelievers with non-Christian habits, I think the story would have been less truthful in its portrayal of the characters, and certainly less interesting – particularly for a non-religious reader.

Christian writers who want their books to be read by non-Christians have to be wary of two other big turn-offs – boredom and jargon. You have to avoid telling the events in long, dreary paragraphs, punctuated in a slovenly way with 'and then'. This is no better than a long and boring list of facts. It is not just our TV culture that dictates the need for short, vivid sentences, dramatic 'show-not-tell' narrative and lively, life-like dialogue. These are the best vehicles of instant communication between writer and reader – the nearest you will get to taking the reader through an experience for himself so that he feels what you have felt.

Jargon is a communication-killer simply because it is so exclusive. To write from a Christian perspective about 'receiving a word from the Lord that witnessed to my spirit' is to limit your readership to the in-crowd who use the in-language. Far better to describe your experiences in a way that will make them accessible to any reader with normal human emotions: 'When I heard the minister saying those words, I felt as if they had been specially written just for me. I even began to wonder whether this might be God's way of answering my faltering prayers.'

Finally, faith

Writing Christian autobiography is communicating a message about God and His people, using *facts* (a balance of light and dark), *feelings* (normal human emotions), *folk* (real people with real responses), and *fiction skills* to bring your reader into the action. If you get it right, you will also bring your reader into a new *faith* in the God you have truthfully portrayed.

5

WRITING RELIGIOUS NON-FICTION

The magazine article

The word 'article' is used by freelance writers to mean a piece of factual writing conveying information. For the religious writer, this can cover everything from a report for the church magazine to a scholarly essay for an academic periodical, and there are all kinds of variations in between, depending on the kind of information you want to convey and the kind of publication you are writing for. Here are some of the most common article types you might wish to try:

Report
If you are describing an event or reporting a meeting, then obviously you must get your facts right. It is a good idea to take as many notes as you can at the time, collect any handouts that are offered and double-check, if possible, with someone else who was there. Decide on a catchy opening (there is a section about this later), then arrange all your facts in logical sequence. In an article, everyday language is more acceptable than the very formal style of committee minutes. So you would write: 'The Bishop of Mudcaster came and spoke to the Fabric Committee last month on the work of grant-awarding agencies' and not 'The bi-monthly meeting of the Fabric Committee of the Parish Church of St Wulstride Saint and Martyr was held on Tuesday November 17th, when there was an address by the Rt Revd Anthony Moorgate, Bishop of Mudcaster, entitled "Grant-Awarding Agencies, Who They Are and How They Work".'

Personal Experience
A personal-experience article is an account of some event which happened to you personally. Usually, for the religious markets, this

would include some spiritual insights gained through the experience. (See Chapter 2 for a full treatment of the personal-experience article.)

Specialist Knowledge

If you have expert knowledge in a particular field, you could write an article which might take the form of advice, or a survey (for example 'Church Schools – Choosing the Best'), or an up-to-date review of your specialist area (for example, 'New Findings in the Dead Sea Scrolls'). If you are *not* an expert, you may be able to research suitable information for a specialist article from the relevant section of the local library.

How-To

A how-to article applies your specialist knowledge in the form of an explanation. You could describe how to do something (for example 'Praising God while You're Raising Kids', a piece on how to plan family prayers), or how to make something (for example 'How to Make an Advent Calendar'), or perhaps how to organise something (for example 'Starting a Regular Pre-schoolers' Service'). You have to remember when you are writing a how-to that you are the 'teacher' of a 'class' that cannot ask you any questions. This means that you must explain everything clearly and concisely, step-by-step, and even include helpful diagrams or pictures where appropriate.

General Interest

A general interest article might give information about the background to something familiar (for example, 'Let There Be Light – Why We Use Candles in Church'), or it might introduce the reader to something which is as yet new to him (for example, 'Redeeming the Plastic Card – Pocket Computer Bibles and Commentaries').

Anniversary and Biography

An anniversary or biographical article explores a topical calendar event or profiles a person from the past at a special anniversary time. The main thing to remember when writing these calendar-related articles is that magazines are prepared some time ahead of their publication date. The 'lead time' – the time between editing the material and its appearance in the shops – is often longer than you might think. You would be wise to submit topical material to weekly publications three months ahead of the relevant date, to monthlies six months ahead and to quarterlies nine months ahead.

Interview and Profile

The interview article is just that - an interview with a living person who is of interest to the reader either because they are famous or because they typify some area of interest for the reader. You need to do your homework before the actual interview, finding out as much as you can about the person you are going to see. This will ensure that you ask all the right questions (for example, 'How did a music graduate become a market trader?') and none of the wrong ones (for example, 'What happened to your wife?'). It is a good idea to prepare a list of things you want to find out during the interview. Take notes - discreetly - or better still, use a tape-recorder.

A *profile* article is similar to an interview, except that you write *about* the person at a distance after doing some research, not from an actual conversational encounter with them.

Opinion

An opinion article tells the reader what you think or what you believe (and why) about a particular subject. It can be topical, controversial or lifestyle-related.

Nostalgia

A nostalgia article looks back to how things used to be - for you personally, or for a particular community, or for people generally.

If you gather together several different magazines and examine the articles in them, you will find examples of all these types and maybe more. When you write a non-fiction piece - an article - you write as an expert conveying information, because you write what you know, what you have researched, what you believe, or what you remember.

Structuring the article

All articles of whatever type follow the same basic pattern:

- title
- opening paragraph
- middle paragraph(s)
- concluding paragraph.

First, then, the title. This needs to capture the interest of the casual reader who might otherwise give your article a miss. If, for example, you are writing a report of the parish playgroup's recent summer outing, 'A Cartload of . . . Angels!' is better than 'The Playgroup Outing to the Wildlife Sanctuary'. However, a short informative label is sometimes more appropriate, as in 'How to Make an Easter Banner'.

Perhaps more important than the title is the opening paragraph. This is where the reader decides whether or not to read on. Make sure they do read on by catching them with one of the following 'hooks':

Question
Which one of the Ten Commandments do you have the most trouble with? (Article about coveting)

Quotation
They say 'there's no smoke without fire'. But I say that this is wrong, and what's more it's dangerous. (Article about the destructive power of rumour)

Shock Statement
Imagine half our village in hospital wards or morgues this Christmas – that's how many people will be killed or injured in drink-drive accidents during the holiday period. (Article about Christian responsibility)

Anecdote
It was two o'clock on a summer afternoon in our quiet English vicarage when the phone rang, and I suddenly found myself taking part in a live radio breakfast show in western California. (Article about the media)

Dialogue
'Well, you can count me out,' said Nathan, our sixteen-year-old, when he found us browsing the summer camp brochures. 'I'm going to Greece with a gang from work.' (Article about parent-teenager relationships)

Case History

Two years ago, Graham Cantrill was a successful life-assurance salesman, persuading husbands to make adequate provision for their 'widow' in the event of their own unexpected demise. Now he's a full-time evangelist with the New Horizons Fellowship. (Article about a local Christian)

Description

Ecton House, once a country rectory of enormous proportions, is now a warm and welcoming retreat centre complete with lecture rooms, dining hall, well-equipped playroom and large enclosed gardens. In fact, everything you'd need for a Parish Away Day. (Article about a parish outing)

Once your opening paragraph has 'hooked' your reader, the main body of your article follows, with as many middle paragraphs as it takes to cover all the information you want to get across. Start a new paragraph for each new angle of your topic, arranged in the most logical sequence. Try to make the first sentence of each new paragraph reflect what has been said in the previous paragraph and lead in to what comes next.

At the end of your article, you need to round off with a short closing paragraph that makes a fitting conclusion to the whole piece. This concluding paragraph might be a neat summary, or a final thought-provoking observation, or a reminder of where the article started – something to 'bring down the curtain' at the end of your piece.

Many writers have found from experience that time can be saved if you try to sort out the basic structure of your article *before* you start writing it. One way to do this is to jot down headings in a list, then shuffle the order until it flows the way you want it to. Another method is the 'spidergram', where you write the main idea on the spider's body, then add as many legs as necessary – and where they are needed – for all your headings.

Length and style

There is another reason why it is advisable to sort out the article's overall structure in headline form before you actually start writing it, and that

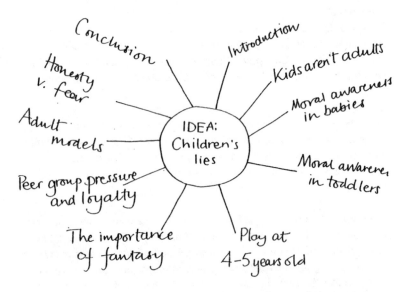

is so that you can tailor the piece to the right length. You really have no choice about the length of your article - either you are told by the editor what his requirements are, or you will be targeting a particular slot in a magazine and will match your article to the required length for that slot.

Beginner writers hoping to break into the religious market often court disappointment by writing from the heart, then sending the resulting masterpiece to a favourite religious magazine without understanding that editors work to tight formats, balancing editorial copy, news, features and advertisements in proportions that satisfy the reader, the editorial board, the financing body and the advertisers.

It is quite easy to assess the length of a printed piece in your targeted slot and also to count the words in your written article. Clear guidelines are given in Chapter 3.

You will have seen magazine articles that have some of their information lifted out from the main text and printed in little boxes. These are sometimes called 'sidebars'. An editor will perhaps decide that some information would be better in sidebars and will extract this from the main text of your article, but there are advantages in including sidebars as part of your original submission. First, you know your subject and how a sidebar can help to get it across, and second it marks you out as an experienced writer.

Sidebars should always relate to the main text of the article, but they don't have to be extracted prose. A list - for example where you need to include several addresses - looks better as a sidebar. Or if you want to press home succinctly the points you have made in the article, you can make a sidebar containing 'Ten Reasons Why . . .' or 'Ten Tips For . . .'.

When you type your article, add the sidebars to the end of the main text. On your cover page, give the number of words contained in the main text, and add a note about the additional sidebars.

The style you use for your article - that is to say, the kind of language you use and the 'tone' this conveys - will be dictated by the kind of article you are writing and the particular slot you are targeting. Check the length of the paragraphs and the sentences within them. Formal pieces use formal language in extended sentences and longer paragraphs, a style which many writers learned at school when writing essays.

But school-essay style is not always appropriate. These days, it is not necessarily wrong to start a sentence with a conjunction (as at the opening of this paragraph) or even to use a 'sentence' that does not have a verb. Horror of horrors! (for example!). Many articles are written in an easy conversational kind of language, without resorting to outright slang - the sort of language you might use when writing a letter to a friend.

You must be very clear in your own mind about the 'tone' you want to convey in your article. Formal language can sound pompous and patronising, and informal language can sound flippant and just as patronising, so always try to 'hear' the language you are using, and moderate it to convey the right tone for your piece.

Not all the article-types listed above need be serious - many would lend themselves well to humour, depending on the targeted slot. Humorous articles can range from a gentle observation with a hint of a smile, through the personal experience described in funny anecdote form, to the sharp edge of satire that makes a point obliquely but with a punch.

If you are at all uneasy writing in a particular style, the result will be forced and unnatural, and this will certainly show. It is not a good idea to use your writing to try to be someone you are not. The essence of good style is honesty. And it goes without saying that this should be of paramount importance to a religious writer.

Newspapers

Newspapers don't normally use the word 'article'. If one of the short pieces outlined earlier appeared in a newspaper, it would be called a 'feature'. But you would go about writing a feature for a newspaper in much the same way as you would write an article for a magazine, targeting a particular slot and tailoring your piece to match it. Most of the major denominations publish a regular newspaper containing features of various kinds, but don't overlook the local secular papers and even the national press. Local papers sometimes like to have a contact in the religious world to write occasional topical features and to supply up-to-date news of church affairs, both local and national. Most local papers welcome well-written press releases giving details of special events in the local churches, and will use them, although they may not pay.

The national papers can afford to pay specialists to write on particular topics, and these are often freelance writers who know their subject and who have the ability to write about it.

News stories are not such an obvious opening for the freelance as newspapers have their own news staff covering current events as they take place. But if you happen to be on the spot when a likely-looking story breaks, you can call the newsdesk of your chosen paper - secular or religious - and offer them some 'copy' over the phone.

Religious non-fiction books

Eighty per cent of all books published in the UK are non-fiction, including many religious titles on the lists of general publishers, as well as the output from the specifically religious publishing houses. Religious non-fiction books include reference books (e.g. Bible handbooks and commentaries), teaching books (e.g. Christian doctrine in various formats), how-to books (e.g. schemes for applying aspects of Christian teaching), devotional books (e.g. meditations on Bible themes), anthologies (e.g. collections of prayers or readings), lifestyle books (e.g. advice on family relationships) and biography and autobiography (see Chapters 4 and 12).

Some of these areas apply also to non-fiction articles, so if you are thinking of writing a religious book, it is wise to ask yourself whether your idea is big enough or whether perhaps it would work better as an article. On the other hand, if you have already published an article (or more than one article) on a particular topic, you may feel that the subject could be expanded to make a full-length book. Check other books in the same area to see what would be required – devotional books and anthologies, for example, are often calculated in double-page spreads, whereas other non-fiction books may be upwards of 40,000 words in length.

Before you start writing a non-fiction book, ask yourself five questions:

- Who might want to read it?
- Who might want to publish it?
- What else is there, dealing with the same subject?
- Why is your book needed?
- Why are you the best person to write it?

You need to address these questions right from the outset, because you actually 'sell' a non-fiction book before you write it. You offer an interesting idea to the most appropriate publisher in a way that shows that you can supply a professional and marketable product.

Writing a book proposal

When you are quite sure your idea could work as a non-fiction book, and you have done the necessary market study in the bookshops and libraries to identify likely publishers, you then compose a package aimed at selling the concept to those publishers. (It is quite acceptable these days to target more than one publisher at a time with a non-fiction idea, but as soon as you have a definite acceptance from one, then it's only courtesy to inform the others that the offer no longer stands.)

Your proposal will consist of three things:

- a synopsis of the book's contents
- an assessment of the book's objectives
- a covering letter.

The synopsis of a non-fiction book is like an expanded list of contents. You list all the chapters, saying in note form what are the key ideas or topics that will appear in each one. You should also say what your intentions are with regard to relevant illustrations.

On a separate sheet, write the assessment of the book's objectives. Start with an outline of the main idea explained in no more than 100 words beginning 'This book will . . .', and include mention of the targeted reader. Then go on to demonstrate just why you are *the* person to write the book. Without exaggeration or outright lies, put the best gloss on the facts about yourself, but be careful not to oversell yourself beyond what you can live up to. Tell the publisher what the competition is, and how your book will differ from the rest. Use the language of the world of sales and marketing – words like 'new', 'insight' and 'comprehensive' – but make sure they really are relevant and apposite.

The covering letter should be addressed to the publisher (or publisher's editor) by name if at all possible. Sometimes these are included in the information given in the *Writers' and Artists' Yearbook* and *The Writer's Handbook*, but you can always phone a publishing company and ask for the name of the person who deals with your kind of book. Keep the letter short and to the point – you have enclosed a proposal and synopsis for a non-fiction book (give the title) which you hope they will consider. You should offer to send sample chapters if requested, but there is no need to enclose them with your initial proposal. Enclose a stamped addressed envelope for their reply (large enough for the return of the proposal, if necessary).

When it comes to actually writing the book, you may find that it develops along lines which are slightly different from the original synopsis. Minor changes are quite usual, but any major changes should be checked with the publisher.

You will find further detailed information about writing articles and non-fiction books in *The Craft of Writing Articles* and *The Book Writer's Handbook*, both by Gordon Wells in this *Writer's Guides* series.

6

WRITING RELIGIOUS FICTION

What is fiction?

At various places in this book, there are sections concerned with the telling of your own 'story' or the telling of someone else's 'story', by which we mean either autobiography or biography - and both these genres are, of course, not *fiction*, but *fact*.

On the other hand, if you have a story to tell which is completely made up, total invention, using a plot and characters which never existed in real life, then you are writing fiction.

Sometimes confusion arises from the different uses of the word 'story' in the world of print journalism, so perhaps it would be useful to unwrap that particular package before we go any further.

The contents of magazines can be divided into 'news', 'features' and 'fiction'. The first two categories, dealing with fact, will contain short pieces called *articles*, while short pieces of fiction are called *short stories*.

The contents of newspapers can be divided into 'news', 'features' and 'sport'. Occasionally, the 'features' section might contain a piece of fiction, but newspapers use the word 'feature' for what a magazine would call an 'article'. Perversely, newspapers use the word 'story' for factual pieces in all three categories.

If all this sounds a bit complicated, don't worry - most freelance writers, whether targeting the secular or the religious markets, use 'article' to mean a short factual or non-fiction piece, and use 'story' to mean a short fictional piece. So if you are checking through the various writers' guides for possible markets for your work, and you see some magazines looking for 'short stories', what they want are pieces of complete fiction, *not* the 'story' of what happened to you or someone else. Article=fact, short story=fiction.

If you are writing books, the terms are 'non-fiction' for a factual book, and 'novel' for a fiction book.

Is religious fiction different?

There are two ways in which religious fiction might be considered different from secular fiction, and these are *content* and *markets*. If you were to write a story with a very obvious religious theme which would appeal only to people with definite religious beliefs, then you would have to target a religious market because you could not expect to sell it to a secular market.

Increasingly, though, the borders between religious and secular fiction are becoming more and more blurred. Readers with no particular religious beliefs are none the less interested in fiction stories based on solid moral values, perhaps because we live in a world where fact is in something of a moral quagmire. And readers who do have clear religious beliefs still like to read, for sheer pleasure, fiction which has no obvious overlay of religious teaching.

Apart from content and market, there is one area where religious fiction is *not* different from secular fiction and that is in the *fiction techniques* used in the writing. These techniques are used in writing short stories and novels.

Ten basic fiction techniques

All fiction stories of whatever length or genre convey a message or a *theme* through the construction of a *plot* and the portrayal of *characters*. These are shown within a *setting* and a *time-span*, and the story is told from one or more chosen *viewpoints*. Readers are drawn into the action through the *emotion* and *dialogue* of the characters, and they keep turning the pages because of the *conflict* and *suspense* built into the plot.

These ten aspects of story-writing are dealt with in detail in other books in this *Writers' Guides* series, but here are some general notes which will point you in the right direction if you want to write fiction for the religious markets:

Theme

This is not to be confused with plot. The theme is the idea behind the story and can often be described in one word such as *betrayal, escape, self-discovery*, or in a short phrase such as *darkness cannot extinguish light*, or *pride comes before a fall*. (Jane Austen used her three-word theme as the title for her novel *Pride and Prejudice*.) The theme of your story will serve to entertain, provoke, warn or encourage your readers. In a religious story, the theme could also serve to teach the readers, as long as the lesson to be learned is shown through the actions and choices of the characters and not spelled out in so many words.

Plot

The plot is the story-line, the framework for your theme. If someone tells you the story of a film they have just seen or a novel they have just read, what you hear is the plot - who did what and why and with what consequences. Opinions vary among writers as to which is better - to work out a basic plot first then decide on the characters, or to draw up some characters whose conflicting personalities and choices will in turn produce the plot. It is probably a matter of going for whichever scheme seems more natural to you.

If you are a 'plot first' writer but you can't pull a plot out of the air, it is possible to cull ideas for plots from reports in local newspapers by playing 'what if?' with a situation until a whole new situation suggests itself. Or you can take an old story-line - perhaps one of the classic fairy tales like *Cinderella* or *Red Riding Hood* - and make something new of it. There is a school of thought which says there are only seven original fiction plots anyway: Cinderella (under-dog gets just rewards after many ups and downs); Achilles (hero brought down by fatal flaw); Faust (the debt must be paid in the end); Tristan (the 'eternal triangle'); Circe (the inevitability of spider catching fly); Romeo and Juliet (boy-meets-girl, boy-loses-girl, possibly finds her again); Orpheus (the gift that is taken away).

You will notice that all these are names of characters. All the best plots are about people working through various conflicts - will they, won't they? At its most basic, a plot is a problem travelling towards an outcome.

51

Characters

A fiction story stands or falls on the believability of its characters. Although the readers know your story is fiction, that 'it didn't really happen', they enter into a kind of contract with the writer, agreeing to suspend their disbelief for the duration of the story – but only if the characters come across as real and believable people. Otherwise, the reader will not say that 'it didn't happen' but that 'it *couldn't* happen'.

A real person is not just a list of physical characteristics with a name. Therefore, to make sure your characters are real to the reader, you need to know them inside out before you write about them – their background, upbringing, schooling (because these factors will have influenced their attitudes), their prejudices, fears, ambitions (because these will affect their reactions to their circumstances and to other people).

Before you start writing, you need to be absolutely clear in your own mind whose story it is and who is your main character. There can only be one main character, even if others are prominent, because the enjoyment for the reader is in identifying, sympathising or empathising with the person whose story it is. The main character need not be all good, even in a religious story. Neither should any 'bad' character be all bad. Real people are a mix of good and bad.

As you write, don't just tell the reader what the character thought or said or did – think of your story almost as a stage play, and show your reader the character, in action, in scene.

Setting

Your choice of setting is important because it can dictate the desired mood for the theme of your story. The decision about exactly where your story takes place depends partly on the plot and the characters, and partly on your own knowledge or research. A 'Cinderella' story could take place in virtually any country, so long as it begins in a convincingly 'impoverished' situation and finishes in a convincingly 'enriched' situation; these factors are dictated by the plot and the characters. But exactly which country, which countryside, which towns, which villages, homes and rooms is a matter for the writer to decide.

You can use actual places that you know – this is perhaps less risky than writing about a country you have never visited. But many successful fiction writers work from guide-books and maps to help them capture and convey an accurate 'sense' of the place. Well-known large towns and cities can be used as settings – using their proper names – with a mix of fictional places and recognisable landmarks lending credibility to your story. Smaller actual towns and villages are useful for writing believable settings, too. Although you would probably use a fictional name, you would still be able to describe 'from life' a street or a building with the kind of detail that makes it seem real to the reader.

Any setting that places the characters in a world of work such as a radio studio, a school, a law practice or a factory would also require personal knowledge or accurate research. It is very difficult to write convincingly about a work environment from your imagination alone. If you are not able to get the necessary inside knowledge, perhaps it would be better to set your characters in some other situation.

Time-span

Will your story span a character's lifetime, perhaps more than one generation? Or will it encompass the events of one afternoon or weekend? Only bring into your story those events which best portray the theme. Previous happenings in a character's life can be referred to as past events without being 'told' as part of the story. Most short stories would not have space to include more than one incident in a character's life. On the other hand, a novel does not necessarily have to have a long time-span – a character can 'come a long way' emotionally or psychologically in the course of an eventful morning.

Knowing where to start your story can be a problem. There is always the temptation to tell the reader all the background before you get on to the main events. (If you find yourself using the word 'had' rather a lot at the start of your story, you have succumbed to this temptation.) This is both unwise and unnecessary – unwise because the reader wants to know what is happening to this character *now*, and unnecessary because anything the reader needs to know from the past can be woven in or revealed through 'flashback' which portrays the events not as past but as present.

You need an opening that will grab the reader's attention and then keep it. Start your story at a point of crisis for your character that will make your reader want to keep reading to find out how the character responds to the crisis.

Viewpoint

When writers talk about viewpoint, they are not referring to someone's

53

personal point of view or opinion. In fiction writing, viewpoint means the point of view from which the story is told. There are various options. You can tell the story as though you are the main character and you are telling it yourself in terms of 'I' and 'me' - this is called 'first person' viewpoint. Its main advantage is that it lends a ring of truth and a sense of immediacy to the account, but its serious disadvantage is that you can't reveal things to the reader which the 'I' character is unaware of, so it is a narrow viewpoint with built-in limitations.

Using 'he/she' and 'him/her' for the main character is 'third person' viewpoint. This has the advantage of focusing on the viewpoint of the main character without being quite so restricted in what can be revealed to the reader.

If you tell the story as if you were watching the activities of all the characters and privy to all their thoughts and motives (like God), this is called 'omniscient' viewpoint. Its disadvantages are that it can seem detached and remote, and the reader is not always sure which character he is meant to relate to emotionally.

Emotion

Emotion is the cement of the fiction story. It is the emotions of the characters that dictate the thoughts, words, actions and reactions which in turn make up the plot. It is the emotions of the main character which evoke a matching emotional response in the reader. If the 'problem' at the heart of the story is important to the main character, it will be important to the reader. As the 'problem' travels towards the story's 'outcome', the emotions experienced by the main character - hope, fear, anger, frustration, elation - will also be experienced by the reader, more so if these emotions are shown through the character's thoughts, words and actions rather than just reported by the writer.

Dialogue

Real people speak to each other, so of course your characters must speak if they are to seem real. In fiction, this speech is called 'dialogue'. There are no hard and fast rules about how much dialogue you must use, but popular novels usually have about one third of their text in dialogue. More important than how much dialogue is what the dialogue is doing and how it is portrayed.

Dialogue in fiction is functional. Although in real life people might chat idly or mutter endlessly, or ramble aimlessly in their speaking, dialogue in fiction must do at least one of these three things:

- reveal something about the character's make-up and motives
- pass on information from one character to another (and therefore to the reader)
- move the plot along.

Dialogue in fiction must give the appearance of being lifelike without being true to life. If you were to tape-record people's speech and then transpose the words on to paper, it would be true to life but it would also be difficult to read because of all the ums and ahs, unfinished sentences, second thoughts and interruptions. Make your dialogue sound lifelike by using contractions (*couldn't* instead of *could not*) and everyday phrases (*Give me a ring* instead of *Contact me by telephone*).

Just as in real life people have their own way of speaking, you should make your dialogue distinctive to each character. It should be possible for the reader to 'hear' which character is speaking by the kinds of words and by the sentence structure used.

Conflict

Conflict in fiction is rooted in the story's *raison d'être*, the problem which needs a solution, or at least an outcome. Unless the problem is resolved immediately (and it won't be, or you have no story!), the main character meets conflict of one sort or another at every twist and turn until all *is* finally resolved, for better or for worse. This can be conflict with other characters, but it could just as well be some kind of inner conflict, such as conflict with the immediate environment, or conflict with inherited or imposed expectations.

Suspense

Closely allied to conflict in fiction is suspense, not just the cliff-hanger or bated breath kind of suspense you find in thriller novels, but the tension and interest which keep the reader wanting to know what happens next, or how a character copes with the consequences of his or her choices. Depending what kind of story you are writing, your reader may know from the start how it will end, but suspense keeps him turning the pages to find out exactly *how* the main character gets to that ending.

You can build in an element of suspense from page one by not revealing certain information to your reader at the start of the story, so that he must read on to find out the answers to his questions – What? Why? When? How? Where? Who?

If you worry the reader by confronting your main character with seemingly insurmountable difficulties in the middle of the story, you can be sure that the suspense will keep the pages turning to the end.

The religious short story

If you are aiming at the religious market, knowing that your reader will have some kind of religious commitment, you need to avoid making your point in the 'author's voice'. This would make your story sound more like a sermon from a pulpit. The message of your story can be as biblical as you like (for example, 'all things work together for good' as in the lives of Joseph, King David, the Apostle Paul and Jesus Christ Himself) but this message has to be made clear through the plot and the characters.

If the message of your story is moral, uplifting, encouraging or even cautionary, without being biblical or specifically religious, there is no reason why it could not be targeted at the secular weekly magazines.

The type of short story you write will depend on the particular market you are targeting. Study several issues of the chosen magazine to find out what the editor seems to prefer. Although a 'short' story can be as long as 5,000 words, you should match your story's length to the slot you are targeting.

Most short stories show the main character dealing with one significant incident, during which he or she moves forward on life's journey, either physically or psychologically. Although you are portraying one significant incident, your story will still have a beginning, a middle and an ending.

The beginning of your story introduces the characters and the setting, and the problem. You start your story at a moment of crisis, remembering of course that your character will have had a past life to which an occasional reference can be made for the sake of verity. The middle portrays the conflict which is keeping the main character from the resolution of the problem, drawing the reader into the story through the suspense. The ending presents the outcome, one way or the other.

The 'twist-ending' story is a popular slot in many secular weeklies, and the form also lends itself to some religious themes such as forgiveness, divine providence or undeserved bounty. However, some themes which recur in the secular slots, such as vengeance or triumph, can leave a taste of smugness which the religious writer may not be happy with. The 'twist-ending' story builds up to a completely unexpected surprise outcome in the last line. But although it is a surprise, the ending must arise directly from the characters and their situation, so that the reader does not feel he has been cheated. (The classic fraud ending is to make it all a dream. Editors seldom buy dream-ending stories.)

What is a Christian novel?

If you think a Christian novel is a book which directly expresses the Christian message in such a way that the reader's attention is focused on Jesus Christ as personal Lord and Saviour, then you may need to do some rethinking.

Today's Christian novel is a work of fiction that can be judged as such according to normal expectations but which *in*directly expresses and embraces some Christian truth without preaching or polemics. The validity of the message depends on the validity of the novel as a good novel.

The temptation to preach is only one pitfall to be avoided. Another is the temptation to overstate good and evil in black and white terms with no grey areas. The solution to making heroes seem either wimpish or improbable, or making evil seem unbelievable or even attractive, is to create characters who act and react like real people, ordinary people with mixed motives. To do this, you will need to have the courage to portray life in all its untidiness, with some unresolved puzzles and untethered loose ends.

And then there's the problem of sex. How real can you make your characters and their situation? Some religious writers - and readers - would restrict sexual encounters to legitimate relations between married partners. Others would say that if extra-marital sex is part of a character's life-journey, then it is entirely appropriate to include this aspect of their self-discovery. But few would countenance explicit passages describing violent sex or abuse. Indeed, they would say that part of the Christian world-view underpinning your novel is the Christian ideal of tenderness and faithfulness.

A separate problem is how you portray the sexual encounter. Some Christian writers opt for the technique used by some of the gentler romantic novelists - they take the characters as far as the bedroom door and leave the reader to imagine the rest. A more adventurous approach is to symbolise the sex act by describing some other encounter which has the same emotional and physical intensity.

There is an excellent example of this device in *Old Photographs* by Elizabeth Gibson (Lion). A young couple are preparing an evening meal together in their remote American farmhouse. They are celebrating the rebuilding of a barn after a fire. While he looks out of the window at the new barn, she opens a bottle of champagne, saved from their wedding. The champagne overflows from the bottle, there is a play-fight and a chase before he catches her at the bottom of the stairs. The scene ends with him holding her very close and the meal is obviously going to be delayed.

The incident crackles with sexual power not just because of the emotions described - love and desire for each other - but also because of the sexual imagery employed. The physical intensity of the fight and the chase, and the erupting champagne, symbolise the accelerating passion of the sexual act. There is no specifically sexual language used, and the scene ends with the couple at the foot of the stairs, but the author has faithfully portrayed a loving sexual relationship in a way that should not be offensive to sensitive readers.

It is quite remarkable that these things are now up for discussion at all, since religious publishers used not to produce adult fiction of any kind, with or without the sex. A quick glance at the recent history of popular religious books will show how religious fiction, which was once taboo, has now become the boom area in religious publishing.

The Christian book trade - like its secular counterpart - is subject to constantly changing trends and influences. There has always been a steady stream of teaching and devotional books, but running alongside them there has been what might be called the 'flavour of the decade' section, the popular fast-turnover paperbacks that do well on church bookstalls until the next bandwagon appears.

For example, the stirring missionary biographies of the 1950s were perhaps a reflection of post-war British buoyancy, but they sank almost without trace in the 'swinging sixties' when burgeoning teenage consumerism and the drugs-and-mysticism culture that followed in its wake brought a boom in shock-horror conversion testimonies. Then came the charismatic deluge of the 1970s with the polarised positions of the pros and cons gradually giving way to an exploration of the spirituality of the different church traditions. It was perhaps not so surprising that after all this weighty worthiness the 1980s saw the discovery of Christian humour. And with the 1990s we are into the decade of Christian fiction.

It is only adult fiction which is newly emerging. *Children's* fiction lists have always been strong, junior novels being considered an appropriate way of conveying Christian teaching to children. But behind that premise lies a possible reason for the taboo on adult fiction. Given the fact that most Christian books come from the more evangelical publishing houses, it follows that the old conservative suspicion of leisure and enjoyment as 'worldly' pursuits has coloured opinion of the worth of fiction as compared with teaching or testimony. Reading fiction is pleasurable, therefore suspect, and as adults do not need a sugar-coating for their teaching pill, fiction has had no *raison d'être* within Christian publishing. So goes the old argument.

Two developments have opened the way for a more general acceptance of Christian fiction. One is the widening of the definition of Christian mission to embrace the presentation of a Christian world-view through the arts. The other is the growing understanding of the comprehensiveness of the Christian gospel to meet the needs of the 'whole person' - body, mind and spirit. If the healthy demands of our intellectual and emotional appetites are to be satisfied, there must be something wholesome on offer for the mind *and* for the imagination.

Writing a Christian novel

Now the gates are open, not just for fantasy but also for historical drama, family saga, human endeavour, even romance. Whatever your special area of interest, if you can write a Christian novel there has never been a better time to do it. Make it really professional by using the general fiction techniques outlined in this chapter. Also keep in mind the following pointers:

Know your market

Visit your local bookshops, religious and general, regularly, to keep in touch with readers' preferences. A recent survey by publishers Hodder & Stoughton showed that today's general book buyers are mainly women in the 22-to-44 age bracket purchasing thrillers, romance, sci-fi and human-relationship stories.

Make a plan

A rigid outline can be a curb to creativity, but it is nearly always good to have at least some idea of your book's overall structure and weighting – how many parts? how many chapters? what happens where, roughly?

Give your characters free will

All human beings are a mixture of good and bad, making right and wrong choices at different times. Don't try to shepherd your characters along your preferred path for them, but let them find their own way through the story.

Keep a 'sense diary'

I have heard this recommended by Dianne Doubtfire, author of *The Craft of Novel-Writing*, and also by Elizabeth Gibson, winner of the first *Deo Gloria* Award (see below). If you can write a 'close-up picture' every day of some small experience involving the senses, you will build a storehouse of images and sensual impressions that can be used to give your novel realistic touches of sharp focus.

Be adventurous in your contacts

You cannot write convincingly about the world as it is if you are not involved with people outside your family and your church. Visit and speak with the kind of people you may want to base your characters on. Then you will be able to portray a true picture, warts and all, which in turn will help convey the larger truth behind your novel.

Be a listener
Conversations overheard on the train, in the street, in the shops, will give you a feel for lively dialogue, some insight into how real-life characters tick and new ideas for plotting.

Be a reader
There is no better way to learn a craft than to be guided by a master craftsman. For the Christian novelist, this means reading the very best novel writers, not just those published by the religious publishing houses.

If you write what is considered to be a good novel by anyone's standards, there is every chance that it will get shelf space in the general bookshops as well as in the religious bookshops. Indeed, with Stephen Lawhead's *Pendragon Trilogy*, Lion Publishing bypassed the Christian bookshops and managed to get Lawhead's novels treated like any secular book.

Writing a serial

Some novels which are published in book form do also appear in magazines in instalments as a serial, but it has to be said that not all novels lend themselves to this treatment. However, there are some openings for longer stories which are specifically conceived and written as serials, and sometimes these do also work as novels. The length of the whole story is usually imposed by the editor, and the length of each episode would be dictated by the normal requirements for the slot you are targeting.

You cannot afford to have a slow build-up in a serial story. The reader must be 'hooked' by the first instalment, and compelled to read on for at least four more instalments if you are to win his loyalty and patience for the duration of the story.

The obvious way to achieve this high level of interest is to use the 'cliff-hanger', leaving the main character at the end of each instalment confronting some tense situation of conflict, and thereby leaving the reader in suspense until he finds out what happens next.

Serials with their cliff-hangers sell magazines but their up-and-down peaks and troughs don't necessarily make for a satisfying novel. On the other hand, if you can interweave two or more threads of conflict running parallel through your story, with their peaks and troughs staggered so that when one conflict is resolved another one is ready to bubble up to the surface, your serial will have more depth and would certainly work as a novel.

The *Deo Gloria* Award

Perhaps the most significant indicator of the new status of Christian fiction is the recent arrival of the *Deo Gloria* Award for fiction. The *Deo Gloria* Trust exists to promote the Christian message in ways other than through the church and traditional forms of preaching - everything from car bumper stickers to Christian fiction. The annual award of £5,000 is given for a full-length novel written from the standpoint of a positive Christian world-view by an author of British nationality under 50 years of age, unless the entry is a first novel. The entries are judged by an independent panel. Details and entry forms are available from Book Trust, Book House, 45 East Hill, London, SW18 2QZ.

7

WRITING RELIGION FOR CHILDREN

Assessing the market

While trends come and go in religious publishing, there is one shelf at the religious bookshop where the product has been not just constant, but growing in recent years. This is the children's section, where you will find everything from plastic 'bath' books for tiny babies, right up to children's fantasy and young-adult fiction. The core of the children's section has always been the 'Sunday-school-prize' books - Bible-stories, children's prayers, biographies of saints and missionaries and Christian adventure stories. These are still very much in demand, but the market has expanded over the years to include humour, 'fact-finder' reference books, activity books, fantasy and sci-fi, and contemporary fiction dealing with lifestyle issues for young people in today's world.

There is also a market for children's stories, poems and activity ideas apart from books. Some Christian magazines and newspapers have a children's section, and there are magazines specifically for Sunday school teachers and youth leaders (*Together*, National Society/Church House Publishing; *Youthwork*, Elm House Christian Communications). In addition, there are several through-the-year church teaching schemes which need children's material of all kinds. Your local Christian bookshop or denominational children's/youth adviser will have information about these. Ask about schemes by *Scripture Union, Scripture Press, Bible Reading Fellowship* and *Church House Publishing*, for example.

General bookshops have always stocked religious books for children, and religious publishers are seeing this as an obvious area for further expansion at a time when they are looking for ways to meet the general market's growing demand for religious books.

As with every other kind of religious writing, success in finding a publisher for your manuscript depends largely on intelligent market study. By browsing through and analysing a publisher's current output, you will be able to establish which sector of the children's market a particular product is intended for. These sectors include prayers (old and new), picture books, Christian teaching, Bible stories, biographies, adventure stories, fantasy and science fiction, lifestyle issues, activity books and reference books. You should also be able to identify any definite theological stance, the kind of topics preferred and the targeted age-group.

What makes a good children's book?

There has been a running debate over the years in both religious and general publishing as to what makes a 'good' children's book. It is very hard to establish what kind of books children actually like simply because this is the one section of the book market where the purchaser is not the consumer.

What we call 'the children's market' is in fact a market of books which reach children through a totally adult selection filter. An adult publisher buys the manuscript from an adult writer; an adult printer prints the book; an adult bookseller, librarian or teacher shelves it and promotes it; an adult chooses it and gives it to the child.

The Public Lending Right annual survey (of the frequency with which individual books are borrowed from public libraries) offers a slightly more secure way of assessing what kind of books children like to choose for themselves. The most popular genres are those which deal with some aspect of growing up or coping with adults. When religious children's writer Cherith Baldry asked a group of junior school children to write reviews of recent books, the children's most frequent words to describe what they had read were *exciting*, *funny* and *boring*.

What makes a good children's writer?

It is all too easy to write a boring religious book for children. The first step in avoiding this peril is to examine just why you want to write specifically for children. Sometimes a newcomer to a writer's circle or creative writing class will say they'd like to write for children because they think it will be easier than writing for adults. This is a fallacy that has to be challenged right away. An adult writer writing for adults has the easier task if only because he is part of his own target group. The adult writer writing for *children* has to enter a world of non-adult perspectives where the time-view is longer, the buildings are bigger and the rat-race is about computer games, bikes or even sports shoes.

Too simplistic an approach – based on the misconceived idea that children's writing is easy – often results in a failure to encapsulate the child's-eye view of life. This can lead to a dire tendency known as *chubby-fistery* – writing from the point of view of an indulgent adult who observes children with affection and sentimentality without understanding that children themselves are not aware of having 'chubby fists', only hands.

Some writers want to write for children out of a genuine concern for the development of children's minds and character. For religious markets, this concern extends to the child's spiritual development. This might seem nobler than just seeking the easy option, but there are still dangers. One is the temptation to use a children's story as a thinly disguised sermon – a device which is, because of its inherent dishonesty, almost bound to be counterproductive. Another danger is the temptation to miss the value in itself of well-written and absorbing fiction as a way of helping a child to identify with a problem, understand it and come to terms with it.

Some writers avoid writing for children because they feel out of touch with the younger generation. This is a situation that can be remedied, of course. It is vital for the children's writer to be aware of the children's world of today, with its attitudes, language and expectations, and these can best be observed and absorbed by mixing with children – in the family, in schools, at Sunday school, in the uniformed organisations.

Perhaps the worst of all motives – certainly guaranteed to court instant rejection from a publisher – is to write for the children's market out of a personal desire for nostalgia, a need to escape from the stress of contemporary reality. Before retreating into nostalgia, you should consider two things: one, some of the best children's writing actually addresses the problems of the real world, and two, a retreat into the world of the writer's own nostalgia is a journey into an alien land for the child.

The successful Christian writer for children is someone who enjoys writing, enjoys children and writes from a Christian world-view to produce enjoyable children's writing of a quality that will enhance the reader's intellectual, emotional and spiritual development. Such a writer will also be making a conscious contribution to the battle against other forces fighting for children's attention through less wholesome books, broadcasts and commercial videos.

Childen's religious fiction

One hundred and fifty years ago, all children's fiction was religious in that morality was paramount, 'Christian' value-systems were imparted, and fantasy was considered heathen. Children's fiction today is written for a decreasing child-population, but for an increasing market share of all books published; and we write in an age when television, video and computer games offer alternative fiction-worlds to a child living in a society which is largely unreligious. And yet, ironically, children's writers find the clock has been turned back as they are once again expected to impart value-systems to the young reader. These days, it is not the specifically religious value-systems of Victorian Christianity which are required, but the 'politically correct' attitudes of the late twentieth century in matters of race, roles and gender.

Secular and religious writers alike share the same 'no-win' dilemma of risking accusations of racism if their stories do not feature black characters, and tokenism if they do. In a world of marriage breakdown and family disintegration, the Christian writer faces the further dilemma of deciding whether characters should reflect reality or serve as ideal role-models. Getting the right balance is a matter of juggling the needs of the plot with the sensitive portrayal of the Christian ideal.

But beware – the 'Christian ideal' is not the same as the nostalgic 'niceness' of the world of the old children's reading schemes, where Daddy went to work while Mummy baked cakes and Granny came to visit with her knitting. When I come across children's writers today using this outmoded and unrealistic stereotype, I wonder if it is perhaps a subtle cover-up for their own uneasiness about the darker side of human nature. The Christian gospel recognises humanity's need for redemption, and so should a Christian writer. It is a matter of Christian honesty to write about the world as it is, with the vision of how it could be.

Childen have no illusions about human nature. Christian adults may bewail their children's acclaim for the hero of *George's Magic Medicine* by Roald Dahl because George sees his granny as a terrifying old bat and concocts a potion in the hope of poisoning her. However, the young reader loves the story because, although the situation is very obviously fantasy, the emotions portrayed are real and recognisable and children need some way of admitting to their existence in safety.

The Christian writer needs to acknowledge this darker side of children's nature *and* put up signposts towards a way of coping with these emotions.

How to write children's fiction

The criteria for children's fiction are much the same as for adult fiction. You need believable characters, a convincing setting and an exciting plot. The main characters should be children, usually slightly older than the targeted reader. Adult characters can stifle the story because of the expectations of reality - if adults are around, they usually take charge. Getting rid of adults is a difficulty for the children's writer. You can't just kill them off; neither can you let your child characters roam loose without adult supervision these days. The solution is to set your story in an environment where children are automatically central to the situation - school, club, gang, activity centre. (If you choose a school, you must reflect schools as they are today, not as you remember them or would like them to be.)

Your plot will need a unifying theme and a problem to be solved. (Today's children still read Enid Blyton for the *plot*, despite the quaint settings and characters.) Your story must be structured in a logical sequence of beginning, middle and end, so that the unfolding of the events gives rational satisfaction to the reader, even in a book for the youngest 'read-to-me' sector. Along the way, you should 'plant' reasons for behaviour that causes disaster. And it is best to avoid flashback, because childen can find it confusing.

Third-person viewpoint is preferable; a first-person account would need to be intelligent and articulate beyond the experience of a believable child-story-teller. Beware of allowing any unwitting intrusion of the 'author's voice' coming in to explain, warn or moralise.

You must know, before you write, which age-group you are writing for. Some writers say they would like to write for 'children' as if the same approach would do for three-year-olds and thirteen-year-olds. Children's publishers work with four age-bands in mind. These are roughly: 0 to 6, the picture book; 7 to 9, the first reader; 9 to 12, the full-length children's novel; 13-plus, teenage and young-adult fiction. Naturally, there is plenty of overlapping expected, to accommodate faster and slower developers. Whichever age-group you are writing for, remember that children understand a wider vocabulary than they use. They like to be stretched by encountering new words which can be understood because of the context.

More important than simplicity of vocabulary is simplicity of sentence-structure. Go for clarity rather than complexity and split long sentences if necessary.

Make dialogue sound realistic by using children's spoken sentence structure with its informality, exaggerations and contractions such as 'won't' for 'will not'. But avoid current slang words, as they date very quickly.

Conflicts keep the pages turning, but believable characters are neither all good nor all bad, so avoid the obvious 'goodies v. baddies' kind of conflict (which is no conflict at all for the reader). Your story will be much more gripping if all the characters believe they are right despite working in opposite directions, or if the main character is battling against a particular temptation or striving to accept some adverse circumstance.

How to write children's non-fiction

Many of the rules of fiction can be applied to some sections of children's non-fiction, for example new versions of Bible stories or Christian biographies. If you are writing prayers, the language should be the natural conversational language of the targeted age-group without being trivial, flippant or slang.

If you have an idea for a 'read-to-me' picture book for younger children, you don't necessarily have to do the pictures yourself. In fact, most publishers would expect to find an appropriate illustrator, after talking to the writer about the kind of pictures their text requires. But you must be able to indicate to the publisher the exact relationship between text and pictures for every page of your proposed book. How much text per page and what size of print will be your decision, depending on the targeted age-group or the particular effect you want at a particular point. Small print can indicate quiet words and large print loud words, for example. And small children can get very excited by anticipating the word immediately after a page-turn. Deciding where that page-turn should be, to enhance the effect, is part of your task as the picture-book's originator.

Activity books and reference books show, much more than fiction, the great changes that have taken place in the world of children's books in the space of one generation. Activity books used to look like novels, whether hardback or paperback, and contain wordy explanations in novel-type print of such things as how to build a model of Herod's Temple, or how to turn old birthday cards into bookmarks. Any diagrams were black-and-white and impersonal. Today's activity books look almost as if they were facsimile reproductions of children's own project-files. They are usually A4 in size, stapled rather than perfect-bound, and even if the text is printed (often it is written to look like a child's handwriting), it will be set in an extremely informal typeface to match the almost 'chatty' language. Any 'how-to' diagrams will look hand-drawn to make the process seem achievable by the reader. Pictures which give information (for example, what the Temple might have looked like in its day) will be a match for television – full-colour, detailed, and perhaps even with moving parts activated by tabs.

When suggesting activities for children, bear in mind the age-group you are writing for, and the expectations of their parents. If any process requires using heat or chemicals, for example, your text should always include appropriate headings, such as 'Recipes to make with a grown-up'.

Reference books, where children find out the facts about something, are no longer restricted to the encyclopaedia volumes or dense text-books that you used to find on the shelves of the school library. Religious references books for children are among the most pleasing and user-friendly items stocked in today's school 'resource centre'. They are large-format, full-colour productions, where the information is presented through a mixture of page-text, sidebars, photographs, drawings and diagrams. As with picture books, the writer is the originator of the book and how it works in terms of reader-participation, but the publisher engages the necessary illustrators.

A market boom – religion in schools

Legislation contained in the Education Reform Act of 1988 requires that every child in every state school should have a weekly Religious Education (RE) lesson which should be 'in the main Christian, whilst taking account of the teaching and practices of the other principal religions represented in Great Britain', and a daily act of collective worship ('assembly') which should be 'wholly or mainly of a broadly Christian character'.

This is an enormous RE input for state schools where religious teaching under the 1944 Education Act had shrunk to very little or none at all. Because of the shortage of fully trained RE staff to undertake all that is now required by law, willing non-specialist teachers are being persuaded to fill the breach, providing there are resources on hand to help them.

Schools are crying out for published material which communicates to the child of today the basic outline of the Bible, the life and teaching of Jesus, and the fundamentals of Christian belief, and which relates Christianity to contemporary moral issues, working from the personal perspective, through the social to the global. But the materials *must* use lively language, and include ideas for games, discussions, activities, diaries, wall-charts and cross-curricular involvement.

It would be almost impossible to conceive of a book for this market in terms of, say, 60,000 words in twenty chapters. Educational publishers are more likely to think in terms of numbers of page-spreads. On each double-page spread, the expectation is that the author will specify the envisaged layout of text, charts, photographs, other pictures or diagrams, cartoons, games and the rest. The reason for this visual approach is not just the growing influence of TV and our cultural preference for bite-size chunks of information; in education these days, the emphasis is on engaging the child's attention and interest to the extent that they will want to explore the subject in as many ways as possible. Education no longer depends on handing a child a book full of facts to be regurgitated at exam time.

The double-page spread reproduced at the end of the chapter is from a Religious Studies GCSE coursebook for 14- to 16-year-olds. Throughout the book, the main text is in large type, and conveys all the main 'framework' information. Further information, comment, question and challenge are portrayed through line-drawings, cartoons, photographs, charts and special 'extra information' boxes. On this spread, the main text section contains only 100 words, while the two boxes (one illuminating the past, the other linking to the present) contain 200 and 150 respectively. A black-and-white picture from a film shows how a Roman crucifixion would have looked. The 'follow-up' section lists reading and activity tasks which will consolidate the learning. The drawing of a file card from the 'Crucifixion File' indicates the official nature of Christ's crucifixion and offers a sample of how one of the activity tasks might be tackled.

You do not need to worry so much about page layout for a book which is to be used only by the teacher, for example a collection of assembly ideas. But the need is still for lively thematic material, with up-to-date music suggestions, relevant and thought-provoking readings (sacred and secular), ideas for mini-dramas and classroom follow-ups, and written prayers.

If you are thinking of writing for the schools market, talk to teachers who are doing the job today and look at new school materials in all subjects aimed at different age-groups. You will find that the text-books has largely given way to the resource-pack.

You get two bites at the cherry writing for the Religious Education market, because it is served by both the traditional education publishers and also some traditional Christian publishers. When it comes to approaching publishers with your proposal, it is understood that there is not time to wait for a single response before you press on down your target list, so multiple submission is expected. As with every other sector of publishing, you stand a better chance of acceptance if you have studied the market thoroughly first, and tailored your ideas to suit your targeted publishers. This may mean sending out six slightly different proposals, but that is a small extra effort compared with how much it will improve your chances of success.

All the details of Jesus' crucifixion in the Gospels are consistent with these historical findings.

(See Matthew 27:26, 32–50; Mark 15:15, 21–37; Luke 23:36, 33–46; John 19:1–34.)

The interesting thing is that the Gospel writers don't dwell on the agony of Jesus' death when they describe the crucifixion. They give Jesus' words and the comment of the army officer on duty, and they tell us of the torn curtain in the Temple.

It is this last fact which gives a clue to the great significance of Jesus' death. What is achieved by this atoning sacrifice (see Unit 12) completely overrides the shame, as Paul stresses in his portrayal of Jesus in his letters (see Unit 18).

The Church of the Holy Sepulchre

People have regarded the site where the Church of the Holy Sepulchre stands as the place where Jesus was buried for nearly as long as Christianity has been in existence. In AD135 the Emperor Hadrian built a temple to the Roman goddess Venus there, hiding any evidence of a tomb of Jesus.

But, nearly 200 years later, Christians remained certain that this was the place. St Helena, the mother of the Emperor Constantine, persuaded him to build a shrine and a church on the site. These were completed in AD335. At one side, a rocky outcrop was kept as the site of Calvary.

Constantine's buildings were largely destroyed by invaders. Most of the present single building is the work of Crusaders.

Today, 1600 years later, pilgrims still flock to the site, convinced that this was the tomb the disciples found empty on the first Easter Sunday.

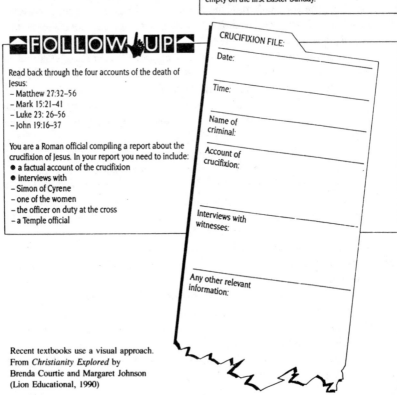

FOLLOW UP

Read back through the four accounts of the death of Jesus:
- Matthew 27:32–56
- Mark 15:21–41
- Luke 23: 26–56
- John 19:16–37

You are a Roman official compiling a report about the crucifixion of Jesus. In your report you need to include:
- a factual account of the crucifixion
- interviews with
- Simon of Cyrene
- one of the women
- the officer on duty at the cross
- a Temple official

CRUCIFIXION FILE:

Date:

Time:

Name of criminal:

Account of crucifixion:

Interviews with witnesses:

Any other relevant information:

Recent textbooks use a visual approach.
From *Christianity Explored* by
Brenda Courtie and Margaret Johnson
(Lion Educational, 1990)

How was Jesus crucified?

Historians and archaeologists provide us with information about execution by crucifixion.

The Gospels describe the crucifixion of Jesus. Dying with him, on either side, were two thieves.

The scourge, a whip with pieces of metal attached, inflicted terrible injury.

● The prisoner was beaten with a vicious 'cat-o'-nine-tails' whip, which had small metal weights attached to the ends of the thongs.

● Then he was made to walk through the streets to the crucifixion site, carrying the cross-beam which would later be fixed to a wooden upright set in the ground.

● At the site, the prisoner was stripped and fixed to the cross – his arms were lashed to the beam with ropes, often with nails hammered through the wrists, and his feet were nailed to the upright.

● The prisoner was allowed drugged wine, as a kind of anaesthetic against the pain.

● Fixed to the cross was a notice informing onlookers of the crime for which the prisoner had been sentenced to death.

● Death was usually by suffocation, because the full weight of the prisoner's body pulling down from his arms made it difficult to breathe, and he would gradually become too weak to push his body weight up from his nailed feet.

● Death often took several days, but the centurion in command could speed things up by breaking the prisoner's legs with a hammer (to stop him pushing up for breath), or by piercing his side with a sword.

8

REVIEWING RELIGIOUS BOOKS

Don't overlook this opportunity

Whether you are a writer of books, plotting and polishing and posting chapters to publishers, or a writer of small pieces, crafting and honing them and targeting editors, the chances are that in your single-minded dedication you may have overlooked the opportunity to be published by writing about *other people's writing.*

Reviewing other writer's books is a profitable occupation for the working writer, quite apart from the fee and the review copy of the book. Reviewing keeps you reading, so that while you can be single-minded in your own writing you will never be out of touch with what is being published.

Most religious periodicals carry book reviews, whether as an occasional feature or as a regular section covering anything from a few inches to several pages. In the constant drive to ensure their magazines are read and enjoyed, editors have three hooks on which to hang an attractive book review, and these are the same for religious magazines as for the secular press. They are:

- the star
- the expert
- the bridge-builder.

The first 'hook' is to have a 'star' reviewer, a famous personality who will be read simply because of who he or she is. For a religious magazine, a well-known church leader would come into this category. For example, here is an extract from a review by Canon John Gunstone, a well-known writer and speaker on renewal, healing and personal spirituality. He is reviewing a book about prayer, a subject he has written and spoken about himself many times.

> There's a maturity about the presentation which suggests it's been digested among different groups - to the reader's great benefit. In fact, the content of the twenty-one chapters would make an admirable basis for a year's course: three terms of seven sessions each . . .
>
> . . . The chapter concludes with an exhortation to exercise the authority God gives us . . . Don't skimp these prayers, by the way: they help you to use the book as a personal spiritual exercise.
>
> *European Christian Bookstore Journal*

Readers who have read Canon Gunstone's books or attended his seminars at conferences and retreats will take notice of what he says in his review. His views are respected because he is a known and recognised leader in this area.

The second 'hook' would be to have an expert in the field, whose opinion will be valued as coming from an authority on the book's subject, and who need not necessarily be a well-known personality. The following extract appeared in a specialist magazine for youth group leaders. It is written by a senior youth worker and the book he is reviewing is an examination of young people's experience of religious faith:

> There's no question we more urgently need to explore than, 'How do adolescents come to faith?' Over the past decade we've seen a revolution in patterns of teen evangelism . . .
>
> . . . So does this book help? I was disappointed initially because it is so abstract. But when I stuck with it, I found many stunningly shrewd insights hidden in there . . . helped me understand the transitions my kids are going through.
>
> *Youthwork*

This time, the reviewer's opinions are respected, not because he is a household name, but because he is nevertheless an expert in his field. The personal opinions of both these reviewers carry weight because each is assumed to have an authoritative overview which makes their opinions worth reading.

In fact, most religious book reviews are written by unknown but competent, readable reviewers who can produce a well-structured piece which will act as an effective bridge between the book's author and its potential readership. Here is an extract from a typical example which appeared in the *Church of England Newspaper*:

> Sharing his experiences of other cultures and religions, he is not afraid to laugh at himself, nor humbly to share some of the wisdom he has learned in international diplomacy and gospel-sharing. One of the funniest stories he tells relates to the difficulties potential Western supporters of IFES had in remembering his Chinese name . . .
>
> . . . He also writes movingly about the blessings of the Christian life. *Getting Through Customs* will provide a refreshing tonic for a discouraged Christian. Do read this book.

You don't need to know who this reviewer is. The writer has given a description of the book and its appeal in a way that puts the author in touch with the reader - the bridge has been built. This is something any writer should feel able to do, simply because a writer reads from two perspectives - the writer's and the reader's. A writer can say whether or not a book works, and *why*. So how do you go about it?

The task

The reviewer's task is twofold. You have to: (i) present the facts about the book and (ii) give an assessment of its worth. The religious book reviewer will approach this twofold task with a further underlying obligation in mind - his readers will also want to know about the book's relevance to their own religious belief and practice.

Presenting the facts about the book is a matter of accurate reporting. What is it called? What is it about? Who wrote it and why? Who stocks it? What price is it? If your review is to appear on a regular 'book page' or column, there will be a house policy about whether purchasing details - title, author, publisher, format and price - come at the begining or the end of the review.

But there's more to the task than the basic facts. Readers want to know if the book is worth looking for in the library or the religious bookshop. So they will be asking some or all of the following questions as they read your review:

- What are the book's merits or defects?
- Did the reviewer like it?
- Will the reader like it?
- What sort of people are most likely to like it?
- Is it interesting, informative, provocative, moving, entertaining, inspiring?
- How does it compare with other books by the same author?
- How does it compare with books in the same field by other authors?
- Has the author achieved what he set out to do?
- What will this book do for the individual believer, or the church at large, or the world outside the church?

The viewpoint

The assessment side of the reviewer's task brings us to the reviewer's choice of viewpoint. This depends on the tone of the magazine you are writing for and the kind of book you are reviewing. There are two options: you either look at the book with the eyes of a typical reader and give your own individual impressions, or you look at the book against a background of other writings on the subject and assess its merits within this wider context.

For popular 'testimony' paperbacks, you would give your impressions of the story and the style of writing, and how these two affected your personal outlook. Here is an extract from a review of a testimony/biography from the *Christian Bookseller*:

Sadly, for me, JW's retelling of M's story does feel a bit sluggish in parts. Most of the story is told in the third person and dialogue is scarce. Throughout the book I felt left on the outside as an observer rather than drawn into the story of the emotions of its characters.

Again, if you are reviewing a 'how-to' manual (e.g. on evangelism, relationships, prayer), you would give your own opinion of how the book would work for you or your local situation. Here is an extract from a review of an American book on Christian parenting which appeared in a British magazine, *Alpha*:

> On the slightly negative side, I wish that it had been translated from American to English. I mean, how many of us own a personal jacuzzi which we can bubble away in with our kids ... and if I hear someone calling someone else 'honey' again I'll scream. Parents with older children may find the book slightly depressing, as I guarantee you will never be quite such a hero to your teenagers as the authors are to theirs.

Specialist knowledge is an added advantage if you are reviewing the kind of book which ought to be judged within a wider context, but it is not an absolute necessity. The publisher's blurb often gives details about the author's previous works, which you can then check out via the library. Similarly, the library or the religious bookshop should have books on the same subject by other authors.

In the following extract, the reviewer is obviously *au fait* with the author's previous works. It is part of a review of *Paradise News* by novelist David Lodge which appeared - perhaps rather surprisingly - in the very scholarly religious journal *Theology*:

> The special humour of Lodge's fiction is in the acute observation of serious worlds: the fraught Roman Catholic conscience in *How Far Can You Go?*; academia opened-up in *Small World*; intellectual feminism and macho Midlands manufacturing bizarrely attracted to one another in *Nice Work*. Now the laughing eye falls on the academic theologian and upon the common search for a perfect place, be it in this life or the next.

Compare that with another review in the same journal, this time setting the book in question alongside another on the same subject but by a different author:

> There are some subjects on which C is disappointingly reticent. In

the case, for example, of Crown appointments, he puts F's general view clearly. But he has little to say about particular appointments – in sharp contrast with Owen Chadwick's *Michael Ramsay – A Life*.

The Lodge reviewer may never have read the earlier novels he mentions – it would be quite possible to pick up the information from book covers, or other reviews. The second reviewer, however, has obviously read the Chadwick book and made the necessary comparisons. But he may only have done so in order to write his review.

The method

This peripheral reading leads us on to the reviewer's method. If you are reviewing a non-fiction book and you are not an expert in the field yourself, you must make accurate notes from other up-to-date works dealing with the same subject, in order to check your author's findings against the experts. For example, you might make parallel lists of quotations under topic headings so that you can make a fair comparison of 'your' book as against the rest. Your own note-taking will also reveal whether 'your' author has been thorough in his own research; if he has not, this will call into question the authority of his book. But beware – any lack of accuracy on your part as reviewer will call *your* authority into question, too!

If you are writing for one of the less academic magazines, or indeed for your own church magazine, it is more likely that you will be giving personal impressions. These require a no less orderly approach. As you read, you will be noting down your own reactions to different parts of the book. The section and its page reference should be noted as you read, so that you can find it again when you have finished reading the whole book.

Some reviewers like to record their personal reactions in pencil on the text itself. Nigel Forde, Christian writer/actor and presenter of Radio 4's 'Bookshelf', prefers to use 'Post-it' stickers – the small yellow peel-off labels which can be stuck *in situ* with written comments on them. They are easy to find, and easily removed to leave the book in pristine condition.

If you are reviewing religious fiction, your own impressions are important, because fiction either works or doesn't from the subjective perspective. Readers will want to know what the book is about, its genre (e.g. adventure, romance, fantasy et cetera), and whether you found it 'a good read', just as they would of a secular book. But because it is a religious book, they will also want to know what part the religious content plays in the book as a whole. Do the characters discover spiritual values as a natural part of their 'quest'? Is religious conflict part of the outworking of the plot? Is any religious 'moral' integral to the story, or is it 'tacked on'?

Here is an extract from a review of a Christian adult novel in the *Christian Bookseller*:

> Although not marketed as a 'religious' novel, *Parallel Lives* has a great deal to say about the effects of Clare's choices on her relationship with God ... Although the main appeal will be to readers of romantic fiction, the fantasy element may give the book an added relevance to science fiction and fantasy fans.

It is perhaps tempting to write a complete synopsis of the story, but your reader is more interested in whether the story is told in an interesting way, whether you were gripped by the issues, whether you really cared about the fate of the characters. If your reactions enthuse your readers, they will want to go and read the story for themselves.

Reviewing religious biography/autobiography or religious fiction poses a particular problem when it comes to assessing the author's portrayal of evil. Usually it is a case of evil (or personal interest) being overcome by good (or higher motives). If the author has described the outworking of evil in order to show the ensuing spiritual transformation, or to make the story realistic and credible, your readers will expect you to comment on the aptness or otherwise of such descriptions.

The pitfalls

Giving an opinion on issues like this brings us to the religious reviewer's most obvious pitfall. While you are expected to express your opinion

81

on the book in question, you should take care not to fall into the trap of using your review as a soapbox. It is fair to say: 'I found the details of the rape scene unnecessarily graphic'; it is not fair to say: 'It is wrong for Christians to write about a rape.'

In a review of a book for teenagers about sex which appeared in *Home & Family*, the reviewer reflects the positive tone set by the book's author without intruding to personally applaud or condemn:

The book, however, is not simplistic, and reaches its conclusions after careful research ... Emphasising continually that God wants people to enjoy sex, and can do so in a happy Christian marriage, the book also covers issues as diverse as masturbation and homosexuality. The tone is both sensible and cheerful ...

The other pitfall for the religious reviewer is language. While it is the essence of all reviewing to give information and opinion *concisely*, this can result in lazy shortcuts - clichés such as 'totally believable character' or 'timely challenge', or paired adjectives such as 'warm and moving'. The religious reviewer has the added temptation of resorting to insider jargon. It might be argued that religious readers will know that 'charismatic' is used in religious circles to mean 'involved in pentecostal practices', but that is not what the word actually means. And there is an important difference between 'evangelical' and 'evangelistic'. Lack of precision comprises accuracy and integrity.

'A good reviewer combines the knowledge of the scholar with the judgement and cogency of the critic and the readability of the journalist,' wrote Philip Larkin in his foreword to *Required Writing* published by Faber and Faber, 1983. If you think you could be a good book reviewer, contact your targeted editor before you start reading; if the editor is interested in seeing your work, he/she will send you review copies of the books to be reviewed.

9

WRITING RELIGIOUS POETRY

Inspiration or perspiration?

Chapter 1 of this book warns of a danger that every religious writer has to be wary of – thinking that your religious writing need not be subject to the constraints applied to secular writing. It is worth repeating the warning for those who would write religious poetry. Inspiration plays such a prominent role in poetry that would-be poets are perhaps even more likely to fall prey to the idea that inspired writing has little or nothing to do with craftsmanship.

Certainly, the sensitivity of the poet to the world around him and the compulsive urge that drives him to encapsulate his feelings in a pattern of sculpted words are central to the poet's work. The Christian poet can even claim with some justification that this sensitivity and compulsion are gifts of the Holy Spirit, who illuminates our perception and fires our enthusiasm with what can truly be called divine inspiration. But the Christian poet needs the ability to use language with such skill and precision that the poet's experience is caught and conveyed as truthfully as possible. This ability is a craft which has to be learned and perfected with the diligence of a dedicated disciple.

What is poetry?

The poet Michael Rosen has described a poem as being like one half of a conversation which provokes the reader or listener to make a response. And, in *The Craft of Writing Poetry* in this *Writers' Guides* series, Alison Chisholm writes: 'Poetry should always make its presence felt. This does not mean that every phrase must be heavy with political or philosophical insights. There is room for levity, humour and joy. There is a place for the poem which is comfortable to read, which is undemanding and does not disturb. But even a brief lyric on a slight subject should possess the indefinable magic quality that makes the reader respond. The poem which inspires no reaction at all is one which disappoints immeasurably.'

You may be writing a poem purely for your own enjoyment, a poem which may never be read by others. You still need skill with words to catch the moment – the idea, the picture, the impression – with the kind of truthfulness that makes you re-live the initial experience each time you re-read the poem. And it takes skill with words to convey that experience in all its integrity to a third party.

Poetry or verse?

Many people who find themselves wanting to encapsulate a precious moment or idea in the form of a poem, turn in the first instance to traditional verse. Verse consists of words arranged in lines according to a pattern which follows the rules of a repeated rhythm (metre) and uses a series of matching sounds (rhyme).

Nursery rhymes and verse learned at school have etched their rhythms and rhymes so deep into our memories that most of us have a natural affection for familiar verse forms with simple metres and predictable rhyme patterns.

The uncomplicated transparency of well-known verse forms from our childhood makes them particularly suitable for humour, where anticipating the rhyming word is part of the fun, and for the ballad-tale, where the pace of the galloping rhythm is part of the excitement of the story. But there are drawbacks to using these predictable and familiar verse patterns for more thoughtful religious poetry.

For one thing, it is easy to be lazy about making your words fit tightly to a well-known metre. You know that the reader will be able to squash or stretch them into the rhythm which is as familiar to him as it is to you. Sloppiness in verse metre will give your poetry a gaucheness which can border on the ridiculous and will certainly rob it of any spiritual dimension.

You can also find that the demands of the rhyme push you into submitting to a word order that is unnatural, just so that you get the rhyming word at the end of the line. And there is a further drawback. These traditional verse forms pull from our memory archaic words which we feel we ought to use because they are the kind of words that 'proper' poets use. You can find yourself writing lines like 'Whene'er those fields I see' simply because you want to sound like the poets we learned at school.

Sloppy rhythm, archaisms, inverted word-order and contrived rhymes will not help you to convey your special moment with any kind of integrity at all.

If you want to explore more subtle poetry forms, you will find that *The Craft of Writing Poetry* is a comprehensive guide to writing poetry of all kinds. In this chapter, I include basic information about metre, form, blank verse and free verse before looking at markets and presentation.

Metre

The word 'metre' describes the pattern of stressed and unstressed syllables in spoken words.

For example, *iambic* metre describes words whose stress pattern goes 'short-long, short-long', *di-dah, di-dah*.

⤫ ╱ ⤫ ╱ ⤫ ╱ ⤫ ╱
The head that once was crowned with thorns (etc.)

Words which go 'long-short, long-short', *dah-dit, dah-dit*, are in *trochaic* metre:

╱⤫ ╱ ⤫╱ ⤫ ╱⤫
Jesus, good above all other (etc.)

You will find these and many other metres explained in *The Craft of Writing Poetry*. I mention these here to underline the importance of knowing that words can fall into different metres, according to where the natural stresses are made. This means that you have to select only those words which fall into the chosen metre of your poem if you are to avoid the pitfalls of sloppy or unnatural rhythm.

Some poetry seems to 'sing' through its words and rhythms, even without a set musical melody. In these poems, metre and rhyme patterns are useful servants rather than tyrannical taskmasters. Many of our traditional hymns 'sing' in this way. They have a kind of melody within the words, quite apart from the tunes which have been attached to them later.

Simple verse like 'Teach me, my God and King' is indeed poetry in the hands of a master like George Herbert, but there are many other ways of arranging your words to provoke a response. You must choose the form which best suits your purpose.

Form

The 'form' of a poem is a formal arrangement of the words according to a set pattern which includes some of the following components:

- a particular metre
- rhyming syllables occurring in particular places
- a particular number of lines of set lengths.

You may already be familiar with some poetic forms, such as the sonnet, the haiku, the villanelle – and even the humble limerick. Again, you will find many different forms explained in *The Craft of Writing Poetry* and also in *The Poet's Manual and Rhyming Dictionary* by Frances Stillman (Thames and Hudson).

Using the framework of a standard form for your poem can seem like an unnecessary discipline. But many poets find that working to a form actually enhances creativity. It can be a bit like setting diamonds into a piece of jewellery.

Having said that, you may still prefer to abandon the traditional patterns and write your poem in either *blank verse* or *free verse*.

Blank verse

Blank verse uses the metres of the traditional forms, but is unrhymed.

This can be a powerful framework for a religious poem. The metre gives a constant repeated rhythm, like the heartbeat that can be 'heard' even in the silence of reading, and yet both poet and reader are freed from having to anticipate the oncoming rhyme. This allows the poet a wider choice of words to create his effect. It also draws the reader closer into the poem and into the poet's experience, because the reader tends to 'listen closely' to hear what is said in place of the discarded rhyme.

Free verse

Free verse uses neither fixed metre nor rhyme. So what makes it poetry? It is poetry because it communicates - provokes a response - and it does this with a sense of rhythm.

However, the rhythm is not metred as in the traditional forms or blank verse. The rhythm is in the way the chosen words sound exactly right when read aloud, or when read silently. They even look exactly right on the printed page.

In free verse, the ends of lines match the natural pauses or falling inflections of speech, or come at a point which will enhance the poet's deliberate choice of sounds. A good test of free verse is to write it in prose and see if it shouts to be allowed back into its lines.

A tightly written free verse poem can sometimes have more impact than a well-argued article.

The poet's tools

If you want to use poetry to communicate something of your Christian experience to others, choosing whether or not to use forms with metre and rhyme is just one aspect of your craft.

Rhythm and rhyme are only two of the many tools available to you as you arrange your words to make the reader hear your message and respond to it. Other tools you might use include:

- alliteration
- repetition
- simile and metaphor
- juxtaposition of images
- punning
- tone of voice
- atmosphere
- pattern
- surprise.

The religious theme

Strictly speaking, Christian poetry is poetry written by Christians, even where the theme is not necessarily religious. However, because every writer reveals their philosophy of life through their writing, poetry by Christian writers will allow the reader to enter into experiences not offered by other poets.

In Christian poetry, the reader encounters the sense of God's presence and the joys and sorrows of the Christian pilgrimage, including the darker moments of doubt and despair.

A religious poem does not have to be couched in religious language or contain a sermon or make aggressive challenges. It will be religious in that it shares the experience or emotions of someone whose life is centred on God, and whose world-view therefore reflects that commitment.

Poetry markets and presentation

Although the general consensus among writers is that it is extremely difficult to get poetry published, it is not impossible. In fact, the person who writes religious poetry has an advantage over the person who writes religious prose, because poetry markets are unlikely to reject a poem just because of its religious tone or theme. This is probably because a great deal of poetry deals with the emotions and the spiritual dimension of life.

You will find Peter Finch's book *How to Publish Your Poems* in this *Writer's Guides* series extremely helpful, and there is also a useful section on publication in Alison Chisholm's *The Craft of Writing Poetry*. But, first of all, a word about presentation.

You should type your poems on separate sheets of A4 paper, one side of the paper only, using single-spacing. Your name and address should appear on every sheet, because an editor might like to keep just one or two from the middle of your bundle for further consideration. You should send no more than six poems at a time, along with a short covering letter offering the poems for publication. Do *not* send the same poems simultaneously to more than one editor, as an acceptance by one editor will mean you will have to request the return of your work by another, a nuisance which he may well remember the next time you send him something. Always enclose a stamped addressed envelope for the return of your work, and do not send a second batch before you have heard the fate of the first batch.

One of the many boons for writers from the advances in information technology is the recent proliferation of 'little magazines' produced by groups (or individuals) known as the 'small presses'. These magazines are not available at your local newsagent, although your library and local bookshops may display any which are published locally. There are about 6,000 of these 'little magazines' and the best way to find out about them is to explore the list of those included in the 'Small Presses' section of *The Writer's Handbook* published by Macmillan. Most are available on subscription, and most include information about other similar publications.

Poets would not normally expect to study a market before writing, and then write specifically to target a particular market. But it is still worth getting to know a few magazines before submitting your work, because you will find that some editors will have a preference for the kind of poetry you like to write.

Sadly, few of these small press publications pay for contributions and those who do pay can only afford to offer a token amount. Frequently, contributors are paid in further free copies of the magazine. Nevertheless, there are benefits in appearing in these magazines. When you have been published several times your name is more likely to be recognised, and you also have the clout to approach a publisher about producing a collection of your poems in book form.

Some small press magazines have a distinctly Christian flavour, such as *Dial 174*, available from 8 Higham Green, Fairstead, King's Lynn, Norfolk PE30 4RX. And two specifically Christian markets for poetry are *Areopagus*, Christian Writers' Forum, 27 Old Gloucester Street, London, WC1N 3XX, and *Christian*, 19 Harvey Road, Guildford, GU1 3SE.

You could also check out the greetings cards in your Christian bookshop to see which card publishers use short verses. And there are many other ideas in *The Craft of Writing Poetry*.

10

WRITING RELIGIOUS DRAMA

The Church and drama

The Church's attitude to drama has see-sawed throughout history. At the beginning of the third century, the Christian writer Tertullian slammed 'The Spectacle' because the content of these shows (e.g. gladiator fights and obscene comedies) was inconsistent with the Christian character. More than that, public shows were thought of as pagan acts of worship where even to be a spectator was to be a participant.

However, by the ninth century, we have the English monk Ethelwold recording the 'praiseworthy custom' of celebrating the death and resurrection of Christ by a representation, with mime and dialogue, which was performed as part of the Easter liturgy.

It was this kind of liturgical drama which developed into the Mystery (or Miracle) Plays of the Middle Ages. By the eleventh century these had acquired a strong comic element, such as in the characters of Balaam and Herod, even during the period when the plays were still performed in church. By the twelfth century, though, the plays were being performed outdoors on carts, which severed links with the actual liturgy of the church. However, the themes were still religious, featuring Bible stories or the lives of saints. There was a general decay from the sixteenth century onwards, and although they have been revived in our own times, they are usually seen as history of theatre rather than as religious drama *per se*.

The fact is that once the Mystery Plays moved outdoors, the church indoors was satisfied with such drama as was inherent in liturgical worship, and took up once more the view of Tertullian that theatre was a thing to be shunned. While playwrights outside the church might explore religious themes (for example Shaw's 'Saint Joan'), for most of the twentieth century religious drama has been largely restricted to plays for schools and Sunday schools which retold Bible stories or pressed home some moral teaching.

The see-saw began to tip again in the sixties and seventies with the advent of street theatre as a means of evangelism, and the realisation that, even inside church, a dramatic presentation which engages the emotions can be every bit as powerful a teaching tool as a sermon that engages the mind. (It has to be said that this new awakening to the possibilities of religious drama did not happen in a vacuum. It was part of the exploring of the arts in worship which was one aspect of the 'Charismatic Renewal Movement' of the time. Parallel features were the appearance of large liturgical banners, instrumental music ensembles and liturgical dance groups, all of which can claim the same historical authenticity as religious drama.)

Professional Christian theatre companies such as *Riding Lights* and *Footprints* have lit a beacon for other Christian drama groups who now have a receptive audience inside and outside the churches for sketches and full-scale plays.

You will find detailed advice on all aspects of play-writing in *How To Write A Play* by Dilys Gater in this *Writers' Guides* series. Here are some general guidelines which are as applicable to religious drama as to secular plays.

Dialogue, action and set

A play is a story, brought to life by being performed by real people taking on the roles invented by the writer. Because a play tells (or rather, shows) a story, the playwright uses the same basics as the novelist or short-story writer - theme, character(s), setting and plot. The main difference is that there is no narrative or reflection in drama; everything is conveyed through dialogue and action.

Writing dramatic dialogue is a craft that requires forethought and effort. Effective dialogue has to:

- sound like normal speech, not written prose
- sound like the natural speech of the character
- be easy for the actor to speak.

Effective dialogue must also be functional. That is to say, it has to fulfil at least one of the following tasks:

- reveal something about the speaker's character
- reveal something about another character
- reveal something about the plot
- engage the audience in suspense, humour or irony (e.g. when the audience is aware of the implications of the words although the character speaking them is not).

Effective dialogue is therefore a balancing act between conveying dramatic impact of whatever kind and not sounding deliberately contrived to do so.

But dramatic impact is not exclusive to dialogue. In his book *Theatrecraft* (Marc Europe) Nigel Forde says: 'The theatre does not rely on words. Words are only one facet of the theatrical experience. Theatre is words, silence, action, symbol: a constantly shifting sequence of impressions. A sudden gesture, a long silence or the slow fading of the lights may say much more than words.'

Your stage directions should include all these elements, because they are as important as your dialogue in showing your story to the audience. Specify those non-dialogue actions which convey messages to the audience in the same way as dialogue. For example, 'She smiles' may add an unspoken sub-text to the spoken words. However, the overall visual impression made up of the set, props and actors' movements around the stage are part of the director's job, so there is no need to say: 'He walks towards the sofa.'

When writing a stage play as opposed to a prose story, your choice of setting is limited, partly by space but largely by cost. Elaborate sets and costumes are prohibitively expensive, especially for church groups. So the simpler the costumes, the fewer the sets, and the fewer the changes from set to set, the more accessible your play will be.

Conventional forms

The conventional forms of stage play for the theatre are the one-act play and the three-act play. The one-act play runs for thirty to forty-five minutes and can be thought of as equivalent to a short story. It deals with only one situation with no sub-plot and probably has no more than about six characters.

The three-act play is more like a novel and runs for about two and a half hours (including the intervals). Traditionally, Act I (the longest) would be the 'exposition', where the theme, characters and setting are introduced. Act II would then be the 'development', with all kinds of twists and turns and sub-plots. Act III would be the 'resolution' working towards the ending.

These conventional forms are by no means *de rigueur* - many successful commercial productions are in two acts or even four. (Shakespeare's plays are in five acts.) A play should be as long as it needs to be to get the story across satisfactorily.

The other major convention of the theatre - the platform stage with proscenium arch and curtains - is not an absolute necessity either. The more adventurous professional companies of the sixties and seventies worked almost exclusively with 'theatre-in-the-round' so that this is now an accepted option for virtually any production.

Alternative forms

Most congregations are used to seeing the occasional short piece of drama in church, often as part of a 'family service'. It can be used to bring a Bible-reading to life, just by adapting the narrative to become dialogue in the mouths of the characters, as in *The Dramatised Bible* published by Marshall Pickering. Or a Bible incident can be expanded and dramatised in a modern idiom. In place of or in conjunction with a talk or a sermon, a short sketch can embody some Bible teaching or religious concept for the individual to think about.

Perhaps the simplest form of drama for church is the narrated mime, often used for the Nativity Play, where the characters mime the appropriate actions and movement while a narrator declaims the story. The interest and impact is more than doubled if you give the story to *two* narrators. Place them either side of the action and split the narrative into short chunks of fast-moving dialogue. This way, you can even put direct speech into the narrators' mouths at appropriate points, which immediately makes the characters seem like living people rather than moving cut-outs.

As a teaching or evangelistic tool, the short sketch has much to commend it, but its apparent simplicity is deceptive because it is not necessarily easy to write. Its miniature form can be compared to the limerick and, just as we all appreciate a brilliantly constructed and witty limerick, we have all heard dozens which are shoddy, obvious or unfunny.

A sketch needs to make one single point, in the form of a crisp distillation of the teaching or concept. There is no room for sub-plot, detour or padding. Neither is there room for character-building. This is why most sketches are humorous or at least light; comedy can work with stereotypes, whereas serious drama needs the time and space to create believable characters with emotions, motives and reactions from which the drama evolves.

And yet a humorous sketch can still make a deadly earnest point. Perhaps the best-known modern religious sketch is Murray Watts' *The Parable of the Good Punk Rocker*, written to underline the sense of disgust and hostility the word 'Samaritan' would have aroused in the original hearers of Jesus' parable. *Punk Rocker* remains funny years after punks have come and gone, but the point is still made - that Jesus sometimes asks us to value and even emulate people we might be tempted to undervalue and even despise.

Humour can be used to show up human nature for what it is, to challenge our judgment or complacency and to present us with a particular responsibility.

Humour is popular with youth groups and secondary school classes, but teenagers also like to tackle serious topics such as green issues. The constraints of children's drama are slightly different from adult plays. If you are aiming at a schools market, the larger the cast the better. Scripted plays are difficult to bring off well with children of primary school age; narrated mime (with possibly one or two speaking characters) works better. For secondary age, scripts with short speeches are preferable.

Markets

There is a vast market for one-act plays for small amateur groups, in particular women's drama groups attached to the Women's Institute and the Townswomen's Guild which organise regular drama festivals. Although these organisations are not religious societies, their drama groups would consider a modern play with a moral theme or even a historical play featuring a religious character or event. You can advertise your plays in their magazines *Home and Country* and *Townswoman* and also in *Amateur Stage*. Similarly, you can advertise plays suitable for church groups in the various denominational papers.

Selling privately like this, you can charge for scripts (although they must be pristine, of course) and also for the right to perform them. The main publisher of plays for amateur groups is Samuel French Ltd (details in *The Writer's Handbook*, Macmillan, and *Writers' and Artists' Yearbook*, A&C Black) whose rates are listed in their current catalogue. You can use these as a guide to pricing your own unpublished material.

If you think your play is suitable for a non-religious group, you could submit it to Samuel French Ltd for possible publication. Within the religious publishing sector, drama is published by Monarch/Mitre, Hodder & Stoughton, Mowbray's and The National Society/Church House Publishing, who also accept short plays for children for their magazine *Together*, aimed at leaders of children's groups in the church.

Layout

Use A4 paper and type on one side only. Indicate characters in capital letters. Double-space between speeches and directions, but single-space within them. Indent, bracket and underline stage directions. Here is an example:

SIMEON: Excellency, we're all brothers here, and
            we know this kid inside out.

LEVI: Yes – and we'll have his insides out if
            he's nicked anything!

SIMEON: Shut up, Levi - I'll handle this. (To
           Joseph) We crave your indulgence, sire.
           You see, our parents have already lost
           one son . . .

LEVI   (Interrupts): Now, now, our Simeon -
           don't tell such porky-pies! *They* didn't
           lose Joseph. *We* lost him!

SIMEON: Shut up, Levi!

JOSEPH: You mean to say that you've *mislaid* a
           brother? Well, in that case, you surely
           won't miss another one!

LEVI: No! We didn't *mean* to lose Joseph!
           Please, don't take Benjamin as well!

SIMEON: I said SHUT UP LEVI! (To Joseph)
           Excellency, if we could just talk to the
           lad, tactful like. He'll be straight
           with us. If he *did* steal your silver, you
           can lock him up, fair do's.

           (BENJAMIN is horrified at this.

           JOSEPH lets go of Benjamin's arm.)

SIMEON   (To Levi): Now remember, he's only
           little. We've got to be tactful.

LEVI: Tactful. Right. Okay then, Ben, you
           thieving little monster - why did you
           hide the nice man's cup in your sack?

           (SIMEON despairs, and rolls his eyes to
           Heaven.)

BENJAMIN: I didn't, I didn't! I didn't take his cup! I didn't even know he had a cup! I didn't even know I had a sack! You lot never include me – Joseph always included me, but you don't. And now, when I finally get my very own sack with my name on it, this has to happen! It's not fair! (<u>Cries</u>)

SIMEON: All right, Ben. We believe you. We know you didn't do it.

LEVI: We never said you *did* do it!

BENJAMIN: Oh yes you did!

LEVI: Oh no I didn't . . . (<u>etc., with audience</u>)

SIMEON: Excellency – the kid's innocent. If you've got to arrest *someone*, you'd better take us.

LEVI (<u>Gob-smacked</u>): *Us?!*

11

WRITING RELIGION FOR RADIO

Radio is different

In November 1967, the words 'Good morning, Leicester ...' launched
the beginning of UK local broadcasting and the opening up of a whole
new market for religious writers. Over a quarter of a century later, there
are more than 30 BBC local stations and almost 200 independent and
community stations throughout the UK. Add to these the established
national network of the BBC and the new national commercial stations,
plus the many specifically religious 'missionary' radio stations, and the
market for religious writers is truly vast.

However, no matter how confident or experienced you are as a writer
for print, when it comes to writing for radio you do have to take stock
of some special considerations which are particular to radio as a
medium. For example, have you ever wondered why even the most
treasured of English novels, when used as radio serials, are always
'adapted for broadcasting'? Why should anyone want to tinker with the
prose of Austen or Dickens? The answer is that their works were written
for the eye and not the ear - and it does make a difference.

Listening to bricks

When you read a story from a page, your eyes scan whole chunks of
prose, sending bundles of simultaneous information to the brain, where
it is decoded into the communicated scene or concept. But if you're
listening to a story, without the written narrative in front of you, the ear
is only privy to one word at a time. The brain fixes the words together

like bricks, trying to build the scene or concept, often with a degree of subconscious frustration because a key word or idea is revealed only late in the sentence or section.

Let me give an example. This little scene would pose no problems if it appeared in print:

> 'Gosh, am I glad to see that!' George exclaimed over the top of his newspaper, as Helen came into the sitting room carrying a tray of drinks.

But it would not work so well in that form on radio. Imagine your brain receiving that information one word at a time, and the possible frustration at subconscious level:

> 'Gosh, am I glad to see that!' ...
> *(Who is speaking, please? And what has he/she seen?)*
> ... George exclaimed ...
> *(Oh, a man. But where is he? And what has he seen?)*
> ... over the top of his newspaper, ...
> *(Indoors, probably. But I still don't know what he's glad to see.)*
> ... as Helen ...
> *(Oh, he's seen a woman! But surely it's something else he's glad to see? It sounds more like an object than a person.)*
> ... came into the sitting room ...
> *(I was right! We are indoors!)*
> ... carrying ...
> *(At last! Whatever she's carrying, he's glad to see it!)*
> ... a tray of ...
> *(Quick – what's on the tray?)*
> ... drinks.
> *(Right! Picture completed. Next picture please!)*

Perhaps I exaggerate, and it's not the finest writing in the world, I know, but I think it gets the point across. If you are writing for the ear, the word sequence has to be arranged so that each word prepares the brain for the next one with the minimum of frustration:

> As Helen came into the sitting room carrying a tray of drinks,

George looked up from his newspaper and exclaimed, 'Gosh, am I glad to see that!'

Radio listeners can't go back to the top of the page or the paragraph. You have to write in such a way that they never want to, whether you are writing or editing fiction or composing a factual report. News and features prepared for the ear must also be written with the same care.

For example, the adjectival lists which the tabloid papers love to use to describe people don't work for the ear. Take: 'Buxom, blue-eyed, thirty-five-year-old Midlands housewife, Mrs Freda Bloggs ...' On radio, you would refer first to the name, then the location, would only mention the age and occupation if they were relevant to the piece, and you would certainly avoid 'buxom' and 'blue-eyed'!

Hear how it sounds

Even when you've got the word sequence sorted out and tidied up, you still have to be sensitive to how the broadcast sentence is going to sound. A radio training manual I once saw gave the following example. A news editor might write: 'The South African Government has said that it approves of a tax on people in the black townships.' But an alert newsreader would point out in advance the reason why he/she could not possibly read that news item. If you can't see why, read the sentence out loud, now. Listen to what the audience would hear in their homes.

A statement like that written for the eye usually has one obvious meaning. Written for the ear, it presents disturbing options to the listener. On radio, you have to be extremely wary of ambiguity.

What to write

Freelance opportunities on local radio and network (national radio) are mostly talks or stories. You can write talks for local radio on just about any topic of local interest as well as the short daily 'God-slot' talk (see below). On network radio, unless you can provide an interval talk for Radio 3 (and as so much serious music has religious connotations, this is not out of the question), the likely markets are the Radio 4 special-interest magazine programmes, the short story, and the occasional personal experience or 'new writing' slots. Keep your ears open for which slot uses what, and a close eye on the *Radio Times* for details of the producer you should write to.

'Doing a talk' on radio is like being a guest in somebody's home, or a passenger in their car. It's a one-to-one medium these days – we no longer sit around the wireless in family groups. So the language of the radio talk is the language of the one-to-one conversation, rather than the lecture. Write as you speak, conversationally. And avoid jargon, especially if you're doing a religious talk. Remember the kitchen table or the firm's car, and refer to 'the things Jesus said about the end of the world' – not 'the eschatological discourses'!

There is a format for a short God-slot which is taught at BBC training sessions for contributors. First of all, you decide what is to be your very last sentence. This will be the 'thought' you want to leave with your listener. Then you think of your talk as a kind of funnel shape. And into this funnel you put such opinions, ideas and anecdotes which will lead gradually and naturally towards your one final point. There's no time for any side-issues. Add relevant material to the funnel until you've got just enough for the timed slot. (Or take bits out if it's too long.)

If you've ever listened to a really brilliant God-slot talk, and marvelled at the uncontrived progression from initial 'hook' to final 'thought', now you know how it's done. They start by writing the end first!

Whatever your talk, God-slot or other, make sure the content is clear and accurate and logical. Use short sentences; not only are they easier to listen to and assimilate, they're also easier to read 'on air'. Speak personally, of 'I' and 'me', not 'one'. And avoid phrases like: 'Many of you will know . . .' Just as a matter of fact, some listeners *won't* know, and they will feel uncomfortable about it. But apart from that, you'll break the 'friend across the table' illusion and run the risk of being switched off.

Before you submit a talk for radio, try reading it into a tape-recorder. Listen to the play-back with a viciously critical ear. Or try out your talk 'live' on a real friend – one who will be brutally honest. All the time, try to cultivate that sixth sense, that invisible antenna that picks up all the implications of how your words will sound when broadcast.

A short story will usually be read by an actor or freelance 'reader', but it is still the writer's job to make the piece come to life for the listener.

The opening of a short story in a magazine has to hook the reader's attention, and persuade him to abandon whatever else he might be thinking of doing in favour of reading your story. The radio writer has a much harder task. You have to grab the listener by the throat (metaphorically speaking) and *make* him listen, no matter what else he's doing at the same time! And it is important to bear in mind the time of day your story will be broadcast. Who will be listening? What would they normally be doing at that time? Are there any children about? These considerations will guide you as to subject matter and atmosphere. The 'friend across the table' dynamic means that the intimacy and immediacy of monologue-style works superbly well for radio stories.

Some technical tips

Forget formal layout
A radio talk is usually read by the writer. Devise your own punctuation to help you write your talk the way you normally speak - capitals for emphasis, dashes for pauses - so that you sound as if you are *talking* to the reader, not *reading* to him.

Write to a timed length
Base your timing on a delivery speed of 150-180 words a minute, but be prepared to have your pace adjusted by the producer. This may mean some last-minute editing in the studio.

Relax at the mike
The microphone is not a public address system. It's the gadget that gets you into the listener's home or car. Relax, and speak with what the BBC training notes call 'informed informality', neither somnolent nor excessively breezy.

Never turn over
Of course you will only type on one side of the paper - turnovers can be heard! Finish a page with a complete sentence, to give yourself time to

slide the paper across the table and get your eye on to the next page. 'Cue' the first few words of the new sheet on the bottom of the previous sheet.

Targeting the God-slot

Although writing for radio is different from writing for print in terms of how the message is perceived by the consumer, radio is no different from print when it comes to the need for a professional approach. You really must listen to the current output from your targeted slot and then write a well-crafted, tailored piece designed to fill it. This applies to the religious slots as much as to anything else in radio.

What are these slots? That's a hard question to answer because schedules change from time to time. You just have to keep your eyes and ears open. But for the purpose of general guidance, we can consider the traditional slots on BBC network radio as being:

- *Prayer for the Day* (Radio 4, four minutes, recorded)
- *Thought for the Day* (Radio 4, three and a half minutes, live)
- *Ten to Ten* (Radio 4, Saturdays, nine minutes, recorded)
- *Seeds of Faith* (Radio 4, Sundays, fourteen minutes, recorded)
- *Pause for Thought* (Radio 2, two and a half minutes, live).

Radio 2 has up to four of these *Pause for Thought* slots depending on the day of the week, including some at 1.30 a.m. and 3.30 a.m. The two night-time slots are by the same contributor, but the two daytime slots are by different contributors. Each slot is targeting a different audience, of course.

There are also occasional documentary series on Radio 4 and twenty-minute talks on Radio 3. However, this is not a beginners' market, warns the BBC: 'With the rapidly changing broadcasting landscape, there are very few outlets for good writers unless they are also experienced and good broadcasters.'

Let's take that second point first. Is there *any* realistic chance of inexperienced broadcasters getting in on network religious broadcasting? The answer here is 'yes', because the Religious Programmes department of the BBC is looking to increase the number of broadcasters who would help to reflect the multifaith nature of Britain as it is today. Within Christianity, they would like to use more black broadcasters and more women. In addition, they would like to hear from potential broadcasters from other faiths. But these people must be good, because network radio these days is a market place of very strong competition as the BBC monopoly is challenged by the appearance of national commercial stations.

The changing landscape

Which brings us to the matter of the changing broadcasting landscape, and how good writers can become the 'experienced and good broadcasters' the BBC is looking for.

1990 saw the introduction of a fifth public service network radio station and the setting up of the Radio Authority to grant licences to three independent network stations and a growing number of independent local and community stations. The idea is to extend listener-choice, but while the concept behind public service broadcasting is that of *delivering an appropriate programme to an audience*, the commercial concept is that of *delivering an appropriate audience to an advertiser*. Consequently, the pressure on the independents is to attract and keep the audience with disposable income (usually via music and news), whereas the pressure on the BBC stations is to produce quality programmes on a tightening budget. This means that the independents are basically not interested in religious broadcasting and the BBC stations have to be sure their religious broadcasters are as good as their secular broadcasters, because both sectors want to avoid alienating and losing listeners.

A writer in the religious market who is a 'good and experienced broadcaster' on local radio stands more chance of becoming a network broadcaster. The thirty or more local BBC stations (listed in *Writing for the BBC*, details below) all have some kind of religious broadcasting, but as it varies from station to station, the best thing is to study your local market and then write to fit the slot.

Some independent stations make space for a daily reflection. Again, you must study your own local market. If your local independent radio station doesn't have a God-slot, you might talk them into trying it if you present them with some lively material. *The Radio Authority Pocket Book* (details below) lists all independent stations, including the newer 'community' stations, which serve a smaller catchment area and provide 'a wide range of radio services of varying scale and character'. For example, one of the listed community stations is CRMK (Community Radio Milton Keynes) which specifies 'religious programmes' as part of its output. Another is UCB (United Christian Broadcasters Ltd) of Stoke. This station broadcasts twenty-four hours a day without commercials, using 'adult contemporary music and spoken features with spiritual perspectives'.

If you *are* already a 'good and experienced broadcaster' on local radio and you want to move into network religious broadcasting, the BBC can supply printed guidelines for 'Thought for the Day' (details below), but they point out that the three 'Pause for Thought' slots on Radio 2 are all slightly different because of the different audiences at the different times. Study your chosen market, target carefully, send a script and a cassette of you reading it, and also include samples of your previous broadcasting. *Don't* send the BBC your ideas for new programmes.

Writing for others

There are openings in radio for writers of religious material who don't necessarily want to be broadcasters themselves. The BBC School Broadcasting department makes Religious Education programmes which are aimed at children, but conceived as stimulus and back-up resources for the teacher. Material is broadcast in series form, everything being planned and written at least eighteen months before transmission via BBC Radio 5. Writers would need to be familiar with the Schools Programmes output and able to write at the appropriate level, and also know something of the way Religious Education and Personal and Social Education (PSE) are handled in schools these days. Write for details to the Editor of School Broadcasting Religious Programmes (address below).

There are also some Christian broadcasting organisations who need people to write material for them. Not all of these groups are in the business of actually transmitting the programmes themselves; some of them make professional-standard pre-recorded programmes which are then distributed to a variety of radio stations for broadcasting. These pre-recorded programmes might be heard on hospital radio in the UK or on short-wave radio anywhere in the world. If you really feel your writing is a way of 'spreading the good news' then this can be an extremely fulfilling outlet, even though there is no financial reward.

The range of programmes produced by these Christian stations is enormous, from travel and sports features to specifically religious teaching. Some organisations also run training courses for writers who wish to write not just for these religious radio groups but also for local radio.

Of course, the listener is not necessarily aware of whether or not a programme has been pre-recorded. So the same rules apply for writers in this field as in all other areas of religious broadcasting. No matter what the programme, the art of writing for radio lies in the ability to hear with the listener's ear. Religious radio stations and programme makers are listed in *The Master List* published by Capstone, and in *Air Your Faith* published by Jay Brooks. In addition, here are some useful addresses:

The Editor
Religious Programmes: Radio
BBC
Broadcasting House
London
W1A 1AA

The Editor
Religious Programmes
Schools Broadcasting: Radio
BBC
3 Portland Place
London
W1A 1AA

Writing for the BBC (ISBN 0 563 20468 0)
BBC Enterprises Ltd
Woodlands
80 Wood Lane
London
W12 0TT

The Radio Authority Pocket Book
Press Office
The Radio Authority
70 Brompton Road
London
SW3 1EY

12

WRITING WITH OTHERS

When others hold the key

Chapter 8 of this book shows how writing book reviews offers the opportunity of being published through writing about other people's books.

Here we look at two further areas where it is other people who provide the key to possible publication. I'm talking about actual collaboration between two people in the production of one book. There are two ways of doing this but, as the dynamics are quite different, we shall take them separately. These two methods of collaboration are ghost-writing and co-writing.

Ghost-writing, a Christian service

Ghost-writing in the religious sector is one of publishing's paradoxes. Although many – perhaps most – Christian biographies are ghost-written, the nature of the genre is such that few ghost-writers are known by name. This is because an autobiography is about a particular personality who is the first-person main character in the book, and it is this person who is more important to the reader. Even when the ghost-writer is known and respected, very often he is overlooked as the actual writer of a popular book.

Three of the all-time 'greats' in Christian book-publishing are *The Cross and the Switchblade*, *The Hiding Place* and *God's Smuggler*. These are well-known titles – the first two were made into films – by well-known authors: David Wilkerson, Corrie Ten Boom and Brother

Andrew. In fact, although these particular titles are the autobiographies of those particular people, all three books were actually written by John and Elizabeth Sherrill. That is to say, they were ghost-written.

Many of the testimonies on your local Christian bookseller's shelves today have been written by someone other than the book's subject. There is no deceit or subterfuge about this: the ghost-writing is usually acknowledged on the book's cover with the phrase 'as told to . . . (name of ghost-writer)' or just 'with . . . (name of ghost-writer)'. Inside, the book is cast in the first-person just as if the subject had taken up the pen and written it him/herself.

In case you are wondering whether ghost-writers are perhaps some kind of literary parasite, let us consider just why someone with a marvellous testimony would need a ghost-writer. Surely anyone can 'give their testimony' in their own words? Indeed, surely they *ought* to do this for it to be a genuine witness to the power of God in their life?

Anyone who has heard the halting but moving words of a new believer recounting the events leading up to their moment of commitment - as often happens at an adult baptism service - would agree that the hesitancy and lack of affectation do enhance the sense of genuineness about what is being said.

But once you start considering a *written* testimony, you are in an entirely different sphere of communication, where any gaucheness is an irritation to the reader and therefore a   hindrance to the effective conveying of the story. The plain truth is, not everyone with a story to tell has the skill to tell it *well*.

A written testimony needs to be put together in a way that helps the reader to do four things:

- understand the historical facts
- appreciate the spiritual truths
- consider the wider implications
- keep turning the pages for sheer enjoyment (the 'I-couldn't-put-it-down' factor).

Unless the subject of the book happens to be a competent writer, he or his publisher will look for a good ghost-writer to write the story in a professional way.

A good ghost-writer may not ever become famous, but he can be a real godsend. First of all, he is a blessing to the story's subject, because he has the skills to tell the story well. Then he is a blessing to the reader, whose enjoyment of the book depends on those skills. He is also a blessing to the publisher and the bookseller if the book sells well because of the way it is written. So seen this way, ghost-writing is not merely a craft, it is a real Christian service.

How do you become a ghost-writer?

If you are already a published writer, you may be approached about ghost-writing by a publisher who knows your style and who already has a subject in mind. But why wait? If you are a published writer, there is nothing to stop you approaching a publisher with ideas of well-known Christian personalities whose stories are not yet in print, or even just with the proposal that you would like to be considered when he is next looking for a competent ghost-writer.

If you are not already a published writer, a publisher would probably not want to risk letting you ghost a well-known personality, but you do still have an entrée. If you know someone – or if you know *of* someone – who is not a personality but who definitely has a story worth telling and would like it to be told, then you can approach an appropriate publisher exactly as you would with any other unsolicited manuscript, i.e. send a synopsis and two chapters with a short covering letter. Your manuscript will be treated in exactly the same way as other manuscripts. If it is a good story, appropriate to the publisher's current list, and the samples are well written in an appropriate style, it won't be turned down simply because its ghost-writer is as yet unpublished.

What are the advantages of ghost-writing? The publisher's advance and the royalties are usually split 50/50 between the subject and the writer, so the monetary reward is not as great as when you are writing on your own. But despite this, there are still two obvious advantages to ghost-writing. One, you won't be working alone and two, the plot is already written.

Planning together – structure and theme

Writing someone else's story in the first person, as if they were writing it themselves, requires a relationship of trust and openness between the partners so that both can feel that each chapter is just as it should be. In particular, the subject ought to be able to say of the book: 'Yes – this is me.'

Jane Collins, who ghosted Caroline Urquhart's *His God, My God* (Highland Books), suggests some questions that partners might consider together at the outset of a project:

- What are your hopes and ambitions for the book under God?
- Who is going to read it?
- What do you want to tell them?
- Are there any other books saying the same thing?
- Is there room for yours in this competitive market?
  (from *A Way With Words*, ed. E. England, Highland Books)

Talking around these issues will ensure that writer and subject share a single vision for the book. Once the partners are agreed on fundamentals, it is then a case of getting the balance right not just in the relationship, but in the structuring of the book. Here, you actually have a problem in already having the plot, because you have to decide between you how much to put in, how much to leave out and how much to invent.

Invent? you ask, with incredulous horror. *Invent, in a religious true story?* The answer is yes – within limits and for the purpose of conveying the spiritual truth at the heart of the story.

Judicious use of invention is necessary to the integrity of the story as a whole. For example, in using dialogue, you will of necessity 'invent' conversations. You should also be using 'show-not-tell' narrative which describes 'character in action in scene'. In doing this, you will use your researched information about a character to make him fiddle with the change in his pocket or pace the room when you have no real evidence that he actually did this at precisely that moment. Inventions like this bring the book to life and do no violence to the real truth of the story and its message.

Sometimes, in order to convey the truth of the message of your book, you may need to portray your subject in a situation which – if recounted factually - might cause distress to people involved at the time. The answer here is to change the location and/or the participants - inventing characters if necessary. The spiritual truth will not be diminished by a change in the historical truth about the location or the participants, whereas the spiritual truth would certainly be diminished if the facts were rehearsed in a way which caused hurt.

Apart from making decisions together about the balance of the book in terms of its structure, you and your subject will also need to have a shared vision at the outset about the *theme* of the book.

The ghost-written Christian autobiography is quite different from the ghost-written memoirs of a soap star in that *your* book will have some kind of message woven in. You will have discussed this when considering the question 'What do you want to tell them?'

Having this theme clearly established is actually very important for the structure of the book, because you will decide between you which historical events should be included on the basis of how they relate to the overall theme. This approach will also help you to decide where to start and where to finish. It will help you to see the importance of seemingly insignificant incidents and, conversely, the irrelevance of events which in other contexts would be much more important.

Of course, the theme is never spelled out in capital letters. As a skilled writer, it is your job to weave your theme into your chosen incidents in such a way that the spiritual truths are obvious without being hammered home by 'the author's voice from the pulpit'. Questions about the wider implications of these truths should also be woven naturally into the story, as the characters themselves juggle with these issues.

In your initial planning, it might be advisable to agree on a working synopsis as soon as possible. The whole thing may well change beyond all recognition as you work through it, but to have some plan of campaign will avoid wasting time on unprofitable meandering and will give both of you a sense of achievement as you complete one section and move on to another.

Working together - a delicate relationship

As the skilled writer you *are* the expert, and you will doubtless have some very good ideas about the best working arrangements and the book's structure and tone, but if you flatten your partner under the weight of your superior knowledge and experience at your first session, you will find yourself trying to prise pearls from a clam! Keep your ideas to yourself to begin with and listen instead to your partner. Try to have that kind of listening ear that picks up any unspoken sub-text which, with the right cue from you, could be developed into a profitable area for examination and reflection.

Lee Roddy, an American religious writer of twenty-five books, most of them in collaboration with non-writers, gives this advice on letting the subject talk:

> The average subject simply wants to sit down and narrate his or her life story. It has been my experience that this tendency cannot be overcome by explanation. So I've learned to let the subject talk into the recorder. Later, going over the typed transcript of the tapes, I'll highlight with a coloured marker those events that seem the high stuff of drama. Then I hold a second session and ask – no, insist politely – that the subject re-create those parts.
> (from *Writing To Inspire*, ed. W. Gentz, Highland Books)

Most people these days are well-used to tape-recorders, and it will certainly make your task easier if your subject will allow you to have one running unobtrusively while you talk. By all means, take notes as well – a written record helps you locate the right piece of tape later, particularly if you can note the rev. count. But if your partner is having to wait or repeat while you write it all down, they might lose the flow of a train of thought which can suddenly light on a 'forgotten' incident of some significance.

If your partner is nervous of the tape-recorder, agree between you to keep it out of sight while running, and talk about the weather and the family until your subject is relaxed. If, once you get on to the matter in hand, your subject mentions only briefly something which you think might be worth exploring more deeply, don't stop the machine to chase up the point of interest – jot it down in your note-book and come back to it later.

Think through the next chapter in good time before your next planned meeting with your partner. Work out what questions you think you need to ask and send them in advance to allow time for thought. Simple factual questions - 'Could you hear the trains from the house?' - can be answered in writing. Use the tape-recorder for responses to questions about emotions or relationships.

The secret's in the detail

If the reader is to 'see' the action and 'feel' the emotion, they need to 'be there'. The secret of this immediacy is detail - not catalogues of confusing minutiae, but touches of realism which bring the text to life. Questions like: 'Do you prefer tea or coffee in the mornings?', 'Were there trees in your garden?', 'What did sunlight do to the inside of your house/church?' will furnish you with a palette of colours from which to paint a truly life-like scene.

David Porter, who has ghosted nine Christian biographies including the award-winning *Freed for Life* by Rita Nightingale, has a useful method for capturing realistic characterisation. Using information from his subject, he completes three sets of small file cards for each featured character:

- details of *appearance*
- details of *speech habits*
- details of *physical mannerisms and gestures*.

He then refers to these cards whenever he is writing about that person, and uses the details accordingly. The end result is that these characters he has never met come across as absolutely true to life, even to those who know them well.

An important part of realistic detail is dialogue. Your partner's encounters with other people will have involved them speaking to each other and, to be 'true' to these encounters, you must use dialogue in your presentation of the story. Dialogue will make an incident 'live'. It should also portray character, furnish information or move the story forward. You will know your partner well enough to 'hear' how he or she might have spoken in a given situation. You will need to ask your partner about what kind of person someone else was - were they shy or assertive, dour or humorous, mercurial or ponderous?

115

Watch your style

Most of your book's sales will be through the Christian bookshops to Christian readers, but the overall theme – the 'message' of your book – should be a message of hope for a wider audience too. This means that you must be especially careful not to kill the effect of your message by wrapping it in language that can only be understood by the 'in' crowd. Avoid jargon phrases like 'living in the victory' and 'seeking a word'.

The best advice, as always, is to study the market. Read other testimonies of the type you hope yours will be, ghost-written or unaided account. Go back to an autobiography which has really impressed you and read it again with the professional writer's eye. Ask yourself: 'Why does this chapter work? What is there here that can help me in my ghost-writing?' If you want some suggestions as to where to start looking, try *Chasing the Dragon* by Jackie Pullinger with Andrew Quicke (Hodder & Stoughton), and *I Wanted The World* by Joshua Hui with David Porter (Hodder & Stoughton). The John and Elizabeth Sherrill books mentioned at the beginning of this chapter will also repay careful study.

Co-writing

Unlike ghost-writing, co-writing does not depend on one partner having the story and the other having the skill. For all kinds of reasons, writers of equal skill and standing get together sometimes to write a book between them.

If they are writing fiction, it may be that one writer has bundles of ideas but very little writing time, while the partner has the time but is short of ideas. If they are in a position to split the writing between them, then of course they have the added problem of coming up with a unified style. This is probably best achieved if one partner is 'editor' of the completed manuscript of their joint novel.

It is more likely that writers would want to collaborate on non-fiction books, however. Perhaps they share a concern for the same area of interest and they have independently thought of writing a book about it. The immediate disadvantages of two books on the same subject are obvious – both writers would have to acquire the same body of information, would have to write the same complete manuscript, would have to 'sell' the idea to a publisher. And that's where they hit the most serious disadvantage – there is not often room for two books on the same subject to come out at the same time.

In this situation, it makes sense to collaborate, to share the research and the writing. It is quite likely that the shared book will be a better product than either writer would have written alone.

On the other hand, it might be that two writers, each with expertise in a particular feld, decide that an alliance of their research and writing makes a better single book than two separate booklets.

Or it might be a matter of balancing shared skills. As a part-time schoolteacher, I co-wrote a GCSE religious studies coursebook in collaboration with my head of department. We both had the necessary qualifications and experience in theology and teaching, but apart from this we each had additional but different skills to bring to a joint project. She was a chief examiner in the subject so knew exactly what must be included and also what kind of activities would best help the students evaluate the information. But I was the one who had time to sift through source materials and who was more *au fait* with the conventions of popular writing.

It was our joint frustration with the inadequacies of other coursebooks that first made us wonder whether we could get together to write the book for the gap we saw in the market. But in other circumstances either one of us could have decided there was a book to be written, and set about trying to find the 'other half' through our various professional colleagues and writing contacts.

With a technical or reference book, it is quite easy to share out the work once the partners have drawn up a working synopsis. Chapters can then be allocated according to interest or research opportunities. However, it is a good idea to exchange chapters for comment fairly frequently so that each writer has an overall idea of the balance of the completed book. Sometimes the way the other writer tackles a particular chapter may change that balance. This will affect the way the remaining chapters have to be tackled.

So, although the dynamics of the relationship are different from when you are ghost-writing a subject's own story, you do still need to have an easy relationshp with your co-writing partner. It is a good idea to

117

have a written plan of campaign and to put get-together dates in the diary. You should also decide which of you the publisher's editor should contact when necessary, so that there is no misunderstanding on either side.

In some ways it takes even more grace and generosity of spirit to be a co-writer than it does to be a ghost-writer. Although a ghost-writer might be completely anonymous, he does at least have the knowledge that the book is his, in that it is his skill with words that has made it what it is. A co-writer has to be prepared for his partner to query his writing or even ask for sections to be removed to make way for the partner's own input. And when the book is published, you have to be prepared for readers to say how they particularly liked such and such a chapter – invariably the ones your partner wrote!

The contracts for co-written books will usually split all royalties 50/50 and both writers should also register separately with the Public Lending Right Office which will ensure that these payments are also equally divided. If your book is a technical or reference book which is likely to be legitimately photocopied under the auspices of the Copyright Licensing Agency (for example, if it is used in educational establishments), each co-writer should separately apply for membership of the Authors' Licensing and Collecting Society which is responsible for these payments.

Sharing financial rewards is only one part of the equation of ghost-writing or co-writing. Strike up the right partnership and this is more than balanced by the shared enthusiasm and fulfilment.

13

WRITING FOR A SMALLER AUDIENCE

Small audience, large market

While I am sitting at my word processor writing this book, there are hundreds of other writers beavering away at their particular specialist project in just the same way. But there are also thousands of unsung scribes out there working to deadlines producing copy for the largest religious market of all. I mean, of course, the local church magazine. Just consider how many churches, chapels and fellowships there are in the UK. Most of them will produce some kind of periodical or newsletter whether weekly, monthly or quarterly. Now you get some kind of picture of the huge and insatiable demand there is for religious writers who know their craft.

Writing for nothing?

However, there is a problem here for many serious writers, which is this: church magazines don't pay. If you are a serious writer (and you are, or you wouldn't be reading this book), you know that writers' circles, writers' magazines, writers' handbooks and writers' seminars always advise against writing for nothing, even if you do have another income to subsidise your writing.

They are usually warning about those local papers and county magazines which claim they are running on a shoestring which allows them to pay their printers and distributors but not their writers.

There are very sound economic and moral reasons behind this counsel never to write for nothing. While writers who can afford to waive fees write for nothing, publishers and editors will gladly build this bounty into their budget and keep their publications afloat on the largesse of these no-fee writers.

This in turn has a devastating two-fold effect on *bona fide* bread-and-butter writers. Not only do they find themselves forced to accept meagre fees under threat of seeing commissions going to no-fee or low-fee writers, but the whole writing profession is increasingly undervalued. (Check any TV magazine to see what worth is given to the *writers* – conceivers, originators, creators – of the public's favourite characters compared with the prominence given to the actors.) Writing for nothing compounds the fallacy that the writer and his craft are worth nothing.

Some Christian writers will disagree with this. They believe it would be un-Christian to take payment for what they see as a ministry using a God-given talent. Some others would say that it is un-Christian to jeopardise other writers' prospects by undermining the profession with their free contributions.

However, this is not a debate which is raging in the sphere of local church magazines. True, they don't pay, but neither are they denying a living to writers playing in a different league. So don't eschew your parish magazine, even if you normally write for payment. Your writing skills could make it the linchpin of your church's outreach to the community, and your contributions may well develop later into pieces which can be sold elsewhere.

You could even find yourself in the editor's chair.

Editing a church magazine

A busy minister looking for a church magazine editor will light on a writer in his congregation as a gift from on high, usually because he's looking for someone who can type and spell. But as a writer familiar with the demands of commercial publishing you can do far more, of course. You can produce a church magazine that is (i) a good read, (ii) a blessing to the minister and his flock and (iii) a worthy witness to the wider community.

But editing a magazine is not the same as writing for it. So how do you go about it?

Assuming that you're starting from scratch, or at least have the opportunity of re-vamping an existing magazine, there are guidelines based on principles which can be adapted to your particular situation. And these principles have a very familiar ring to them. They are:

- Know your reader
- Target your reader
- Reach your reader
- Win your reader.

Know your reader

You need to establish exactly who the magazine is for. Is it for the church attenders or the wider community? Or both? If the magazine is aimed at the worshipping congregation, are there more women than men? Are the worshippers generally older or younger than the wider community? What do you think would be the preferred daily newspaper? Are you producing a magazine for reluctant readers who normally get their information from TV? Or for those who actually prefer print?

Similar questions have to be asked if your magazine is aimed at the wider community rather than the actual church attenders. For example, is the local housing largely owner-occupied, council accommodation, bedsits? Do people stay for generations or move on quickly? Are there particular social considerations – one-parent families, unemployment, dominant industry, university? Again, an estimate of the local residents' preferred daily newspaper is useful. (Newsagents are usually willing to tell you their ordering patterns.)

The answers to questions such as these will affect your magazine's content and style. Any topics covered must be relevant to the identified readership and presented in an accessible way. The reluctant reader needs to be coaxed with eye-catching headlines over short human-interest pieces written in simple sentences. The university professor will be attracted to pages of neat type without distracting headings.

What if you're trying to please both in a genuinely mixed situation? The professor will be more likely to put up with a magazine aimed at the reluctant reader – the reverse won't work. But maybe you should use the magazine to direct your academics on to meatier stuff by including book reviews, so they don't feel overlooked.

Target your reader

When you've decided who your readers are, by and large, the next thing is to target your reader with the most appropriate product in terms of design and frequency.

The way a magazine looks can dictate whether or not the supposed reader actually picks it up and reads it. Just about everyone will pick up a large full-colour coffee-table glossy in anticipation of finding something interesting. But not many churches could – or would – come up with the enormous expense of such a publication on a regular basis. It could even spark a hostile reaction from people who think the money could have been better spent on worthier causes. It is a fact that charities get better results from publicity using black-and-white photographs rather than colour. On the other hand, perhaps there is a place for a high-class high-cost church publication as a one-off? For instance, a parish profile for distribution before a mission, or possibly when there's been a change of minister or to mark the opening of a new building?

Sensible costing is important, as we shall see, but this should not be the only determining factor. A cheaply produced duplicated magazine typed on to wax stencils with no illustrations is all right for a really committed readership anxious to find out what's been written for and about the 'in-crowd' that they belong to. This 'in-crowd' could be a small congregation; it could equally well be a whole village community where there is a similar sense of being 'us'.

A less committed readership will not be so curious. They are more likely to want to pick up and explore a more visual magazine, with pictures, borders, 'clip-art' (photocopiable pictures and motifs), diagrams, cartoons and even photographs. This requires different reproduction methods – photocopying if numbers are small, or lithoprinting for longer runs. Both methods allow the editor to decide what goes where on each page and to do the actual typing, drawing and pasting-in of pictures. These layout jobs are either done physically on the table-top with paper and paste, or electronically on the computer screen (i.e. desktop publishing or DTP).

Some church magazines are still sent off to the printers in neat handwriting to be returned in expensive type-set print, but there's no real advantage in this method, given the quality of reproduction from photocopying or lithoprinting and their facility for home-brew illustrations.

To some extent, your identified readership and method of reproduction will dictate frequency of publication. In the old days of letter-press, small printers often wanted copy six weeks before publication date. Today, a news-sheet can be photocopied on the day of distribution. Other considerations are how much you've got to say and what else is being published by your church. Many churches have news, views and reports in a monthly magazine, and 'top up' with things like this week's meetings, Bible readings and prayer requests on a sheet given out each Sunday in church.

Reach your reader

If your readers are affected by the magazine's appearance, they are no less affected by the way it gets to them. Distribution methods vary from church to church. They also vary in the 'message' they convey, which of course will be part of the magazine's message as a whole.

Anything left in piles at the back of church is subconsciously assumed to be of no importance, although named copies will usually be collected. Perhaps it would be better for your church members to deliver the magazine to every home in the area? This sounds like the ideal, but remember that the current tendency among the general populace to toss all unsolicited freebies in the bin means that an 'every door' church production has got to be hyper-attractive to counter this. Similarly, letter-box deliveries to paid-up subscribers are easily put aside and forgotten.

The very best distribution method if you want your magazine not just delivered, but opened and read, is to ring the door-bell and hand it over personally. If the church team can't cope with personal visits and hand-over, home deliveries are best received from personally addressed envelopes. Ordinary human pride makes sure we open an envelope with our name on it. But while this is a nice touch for small-circulation magazines, personalising envelopes for the whole district is probably a dream beyond the resources of most churches.

Win your reader

When all comes to all, it's what's inside your magazine that makes the reader say: 'Gosh, this is good! I must make sure I don't miss future issues!' In short, you've got to win your reader's attention, action, reaction, response, with exactly the right kind of writing style.

Win your reader with *accuracy*. Obviously, accurate spelling and accordance with the usual rules of grammar are universal necessities, as are the avoidance of clichés and religious jargon – both are after all just lazy substitutes for crispness of thought and expression. Win your reader with clarity. Don't use fatuous phrases where one word will suffice: 'at this moment in time' means 'now'. When in doubt, use the *Good Word Guide* published by Bloomsbury.

Insistence on these basics will not erase each writer's personal style, nor should it. Many readers will know your writers and they will want to 'hear' them 'speak'.

On the other hand, as editor you should establish and infuse a recognisable 'house style' so that each issue of your magazine gets a positive welcome as something consistent and reliable. So, win your reader with consistency. Decide your policy – and stick to it – on things like how dates will be presented. Is it to be February 15th, Feb 15, 15th February or 15 Feb? Will you use Rev. or Revd? Summarise or summarize? Saint or St. Or St? Single or double quotation marks?

Win your reader with *interest*. So many church magazines carry accounts of past meetings which are written to a 'report' formula with such a high turn-off potential that one wonders how the genre has survived for so long. I mean this kind of thing:

The Men's Fellowship met at 10 a.m. on Saturday November 24th, when a most interesting day was spent at Nutworth Abbey. The trip was arranged by Mr G. Smith, who was cordially thanked by Mr E. Bagshaw during the tea which was kindly provided by the monks.

Such a report, while basically accurate, tells the reader much that he does not want to know (like the meeting time) but leaves out so much that he does want to know. Why did they go to a monastery? What did this 'most interesting day' consist of? Who is this Mr G. Smith? Is he new? And is that Eric Bagshaw or his father Ernie?

There is a danger, though, of letting the pendulum swing too far the other way. Non-writers producing something for print sometimes opt for 'story-style' - setting the scene, introducing the characters, developing the plot and resolving everything right at the end:

About four or five weeks before Christmas some of the men who meet every week - or thereabouts - at the Men's Fellowship were discussing whether the old religious communities who live in monasteries and convents have any relevance in today's world. We had a new member that evening, Mr Smith, and he suggested a trip to Nut- worth Abbey to see what a monk's life is like, and he even offered to make the arrangements if the Fellowship wanted to go. As you can imagine, yours truly was glad to hear this, as I usually have the task of planning the programme and making the arrangements. . . .

While your reader will be bored by a dusty report, when he is reading anything other than fiction he wants his information in 'news' form. His subconscious is wanting clear answers to specific questions: Who? Where? When? What? How? Why? Today's news as reported in our newspapers is more about people than facts and figures, and this should dictate the style of the write-up:

Twenty of our Men's Fellowship went to Nutworth Abbey last month and spent a day scrubbing floors, singing hymns and eating in silence. The venture was arranged by George Smith - one of our newer members - so that ordinary church people could find out for themselves what life is like for the modern monk. . . .

It is unreasonable to expect non-writers submitting reports to have the necessary skills at their fingertips, so the tactful editor needs to establish the right to re-write. You may come across a contributor who objects to this. Very often it is the minister, in defence of his theology! So long as the rest of the magazine is a really good read, one unedited article won't make too much difference. And you can always redress the balance by using ready-written articles supplied by one of the resource agencies.

Every church magazine editor should know about these angels of mercy. Some supply a complete printed 'inset' of material to be stapled into your own magazine. Others supply well-written topical, seasonal or devotional articles in A4 and A3 format ready for pasting straight on to the page, with accompanying ready 'screened' photographs (for use with photocopiers), and professional 'clip-art' drawings, cartoons, puzzles, hints and fillers. You can also buy pre-printed outside covers to add to the professional finish. You will find a list of useful addresses at the end of this chapter.

How is it financed?

When it comes to paying the costs of producing a church magazine, there are only three sources of income and they are church funds, the readers or advertisers. Or you could opt for a combination of these sources.

If your church has an outreach policy as part of its budgeting strategy, your magazine could be paid for out of church funds and distributed free. You would need to assess what the likely cost of production would be for a year and also whether costs could be expected to be kept at the proposed level after that, so that the church treasurer can budget accordingly.

If this is not an option, you could sell your magazine, either at a price per copy or by annual subscription. But this would only be reasonable for church attenders and supporters, not for the whole community. Again, you would need to assess the likely cost of production for a year, and set a cover price high enough to pay the bills but not so high as to deter would-be purchasers. If the sums don't add up and the cover price looks prohibitive, then you would need to look for income from advertisers.

If your magazine also serves as a community newsletter with items from local organisations such as the darts club or the WI, you could reasonably expect some financial support from these groups. In addition, local tradespeople will often advertise in church magazines as a gesture of support for the church or the community rather than in the expectation of seeing increasing sales. But this does mean that they will not pay the same sort of price for space in your magazine as they would for space in the local paper.

One way of including as many tradespeople as possible - and thereby bringing in as many donations as possible - is to include a 'Directory' in your magazine. This could be compiled at the beginning of the year and either pre-printed for the whole year, or kept on disk if you use DTP.

If you prefer to use display advertising, this can be done very simply by adapting the advertiser's business card. Display ads are worth more, in terms of their effectiveness for the advertiser, according to where they appear in your magazine. This means that you can charge more for ads that go in the best positions.

The back cover is 'top price', because it can be seen instantly without the magazine even being opened. However, you might treasure this facility for your own material so think twice before you allocate it to advertising. Inside, ads which appear next to editorial copy are worth more than ads lumped together on a page. But again, you need to think about this, and be sure that the reader will know what is an ad and what is coming from the church. And wherever an ad goes, there may be some messages your church would not wish to carry, such as those promoting alcohol, tobacco or betting.

One useful arrangement for display ads is to assemble them together on two sides of a sheet which will form four pages of your magazine, for example two sides of A4 in an A5 magazine. The ads will then appear in complete pages, but spaced around pages of editorial copy. The main advantage of this arrangement is that you can pre-print a full year's set of ad pages as one job, using colour – which you would not normally use in your ordinary issue-by-issue copy.

Sometimes, businesses who would not normally advertise can still be persuaded to give financial support through sponsorship. The idea here is to ask a local firm to sponsor the production cost of one page of your magazine in return for an acknowledgment on that page. You would of course make sure that all advertisers receive free copies of each issue.

Getting enough advertisers to provide the necessary funding for your magazine may seem like a daunting task. But the good news is that advertisers are much more likely to buy space in a magazine that is going to be delivered to every house in the district. This means you have a real chance of getting your message into every home through a magazine that is wholly financed by advertising.

Having said that, because a magazine of this sort is so very dependent on the advertisers, who will quite naturally expect a high standard of efficiency in return for their money, you would be well advised to find someone who will act as 'Advertising Manager' while you get on with the editing.

With your own writing skills, your understanding of the general magazine market and the help of the specialist resource agencies and an advertising manager, there's no reason why you shouldn't put together a church magazine that is self-financing or at least properly underwritten, with a message that leaps off the page and leaves the reader looking forward to the next issue.

Here are some addresses you might find useful, both as an editor and – in the case of the 'insets' – as a freelance contributor:

Insets
Home Words and *Church News*
Home Words Publishing
P.O. Box 44
Guildford GU1 1XL

The Sign
Chansitor Publications Ltd
16 Blyburgate
Beccles
Suffolk NR34 9TD

News Extra
Appleford House
Appleford
Abingdon
Oxfordshire OX14 4PB

Ready-written material
Church News Service
37b New Cavendish Street
London W1M 8JR

Release Nationwide
Manchester City Mission
18 Mount Street
Manchester M2 3NN

Clip-art
Dover Clip-Art Series
The Daybreak Press Ltd

4b High Street
Bassingham
Lincoln LN5 9JZ

Instant Art Series
Palm Tree Press
Rattlesden
Bury St Edmunds
Suffolk IP30 0SJ

Classy Clip Art
Group Books/Scripture Press
Raans Road
Amersham-on-the-Hill
Bucks HP6 6JQ

Youth Clip Art Series
The Office London Ltd
Unit C
42 Dace Road
London E3 2NG

Covers
Chansitor Publications Ltd
16 Blyburgate
Beccles
Suffolk NR34 9TD

Bible Lands Society
P.O. Box 50
High Wycombe
Bucks HP15 7QU

Editor's Handbooks
How to Produce a Church Magazine by John Cole
published by
Palm Tree Press
Rattlesden

Bury St Edmunds
Suffolk IP30 0SJ

Write to the Point by Ken Jackson and Stephen H. Clark
published by
Jay Books
30 The Boundary
Langton Green
Tunbridge Wells
Kent TN3 0YB

14

WRITING RELIGION FOR A LARGER AUDIENCE

Two further markets for religious writers

Much of this book - published in the UK - has been concerned with helping the aspiring religious writer to get into print in the domestic religious market. But to leave it at that would be to ignore two other promising areas, both of which are open to UK religious writers and are likely to offer better financial reward than the UK religious markets. One is the overseas religious market and the other is the domestic secular market.

The overseas market

By 'overseas' I mean, of course, English-speaking foreign markets where language is no barrier to sharing what you have to say. That is not to say that language is the only consideration when you are thinking about writing for overseas markets. What about the possible difficulties in making your writing relevant to readers in cultures different to our own? Obviously, you cannot ignore this aspect of writing for foreign outlets, but the thing to remember is that human experience and emotion in response to God's dealings with His people has a universality which can transcend cultural barriers.

An even more obvious problem in writing for foreign markets is finding out about publications and doing your market study. If you are able to travel widely and pick up lots of books and magazines to bring home, that would be a very satisfying 'hands-on' way of doing your necessary research. But this option is not open to most of us. So how does the UK religious writer go about researching for foreign markets?

There is a chink of light in the English-language publishers listed in the Africa, Australia, Canada, Republic of Ireland, New Zealand and South Africa sections of the *Writers' & Artists' Yearbook*, but by far the largest overseas religious market is in the United States. Fortunately, there are specific publications available to help you with your market research here.

The American religious market

Writer's Market is a large hardback book published annually which lists US magazine and book publishers and gives detailed information about their products and their current requirements. It is an American publication, but it is available from Freelance Press Services, Cumberland House, Lissadel Street, Salford, M6 6GG. The price varies from year to year according to the rate of exchange between dollars and sterling – the price as I write is $25.95, £19.95 from the UK suppliers. This sounds an enormous amount, I know, but one article sold to a US magazine could more than pay for it.

Book publishers are listed in alphabetical order, so you would have to work through the section highlighting those that take religious material. But the magazine publishers are all listed under subjects which means that you have instant access to nearly one hundred religious titles.

In both sections, the information given is very full and extremely specific. A typical entry in the 'Book Publishers' section lists the following details, and a good deal more besides:

- Publisher's name, address and telephone number
- Editors' names
- Names of imprints
- Type of product – hardback, paperback, originals or reprints
- Number of titles published per year
- Percentage of titles from first-time authors
- Percentage of titles from unagented authors
- Royalty percentages

- Average advance
- Time between acceptance and publication
- Policy on simultaneous submissions
- Time taken to report on submitted manuscripts
- Tips about requirements and targeted readerships.

And an entry from the 'Consumer/Religious' magazines section lists the following details:

- Magazine's name
- Address, telephone and fax numbers
- Editor's name
- Percentage of material freelance-written
- Confirmation that they work with new writers
- Description of magazine
- Date of establishment
- Circulation
- Payment on acceptance
- Time between acceptance and publication
- Byline given
- Rights purchased
- Lead time for seasonal material
- Time taken to report on submitted manuscripts
- Pieces required
- Number purchased per year
- Lengths
- Payment per word
- Tips (direct quote from editor) about the tone of the magazine, and about viewpoints for personal-experience articles.

Most of the magazines suggest you write for copies, and some of the book publishers also suggest you write for their book catalogue to get some idea of what they are doing. You might find that your local Christian bookshop has copies of some American catalogues. If you write for samples or catalogues, you will need to send postage.

The usual system for enclosing postage for the return of information or your rejected manuscript (it can happen!) is to use International Reply Coupons (IRCs) which can be purchased at any main Post Office. These can be exchanged in any country for stamps equivalent to the minimum postage required for a letter sent from that country to the UK. (You would need to ask at the Post Office how many IRCs would be the equivalent of the overseas rate for a package requiring the ten first-class US stamps requested for internal US mailing.)

Most of the religious magazines listed in *Writer's Market* offer sample copies to would-be contributors, and it would be wise to ask for a sample copy before sending a manuscript, to make sure you have some idea – albeit very restricted – of the 'tone' of the magazine as well as the specific requirements such as topic and length.

If you are serious about writing for the US religious market, there are some other books which might help you. *Writing to Inspire*, edited by William Gentz, was first published in America but was later issued in the UK by Highland Books and is available from Freelance Press Service. The book is a collection of articles about religious writing and includes a lot of practical advice, no specific up-to-date market information but some useful general guidelines.

Specific information listing over 800 markets is contained in the hefty annual paperback *Christian Writers' Market Guide* by Sally E. Stuart. The price as I write is $18.95, but a letter enclosing an IRC and requesting details of overseas mailing can be sent direct to the author: Sally E. Stuart, 17768 SW Pointe Forest Ct, Aloha, OR 97006, USA. This book is more than a list of publishers and their requirements: the author has actually scoured hundreds of periodicals and listed titles which take particular topics, and the lists are sub-divided down to the clearest specific categories. For example, for short-story markets the magazine titles are listed under sections headed Adult, Adventure, Biblical, Fantasy, Frontier, Frontier/Romance, Historical, Historical/Romance, Humorous, Juvenile, Literary, Mainstream, Mystery, Mystery/Romance, Parables, Plays, Romance, Science Fiction, Skits, Teen/Young Adult. And then most of these lists are further subdivided under the headings Children, Teen/Young Adult and Adult.

Another helpful book available direct from the author is *Ministry and Marketing* by Marlene Bagnull, a well-known US religious-writing tutor. The price as I write is $7.95, but again I would suggest you write first (with IRC) to get overseas mailing details: Marlene Bagnull, 316 Blanchard Road, Drexel Hill, PA 19026, USA.

The kinds of writing you can expect to sell to US markets include short stories of all kinds (see above), plus devotional pieces, personal-experience articles, inspirational articles, self-help articles, marriage and family articles, Bible teaching, profiles, interviews, testimonies, poetry, humour and fillers. The kinds of US religious periodical to which you can expect to sell these pieces include prestige glossies, daily devotional magazines, church and Sunday School take-home papers, newspapers, education magazines, singles' and senior citizens' magazines, women's magazines, family magazines, denominational magazines, leaders' magazines and writing magazines. These are the many types of US religious periodicals looking for religious writing. It's a vast market, and wide open to the UK religious writer.

The UK secular market

The other sales opportunity that religious writers ought to be aware of is the UK secular market. Time was when several secular weekly and monthly magazines carried a regular devotional article, but the changing expectations of our post-Christian society have made these pieces all but extinct. Where they remain they are written by 'big names' who are well-known to a secular readership. So there is no opening in the secular press for the traditional religious article.

However, there are still plenty of openings for the religious writer who cares to look for them and is prepared to write for today's market rather than yesterday's. For example, newspapers, general magazines, women's magazines, and trade and house magazines all provide possibilities for opinion articles on relevant social issues such as marriage, divorce and family breakdown, abortion and euthanasia, fertility treatment and genetic engineering, individual achievement and community responsibility. Without resorting to Bible-bashing, the skilled Christian writer can bring in the religious angle on topics where 'values' are being debated.

Travel, cookery, health and craft pieces can also offer a chance to inform the reader about some religious allusion or context they may not otherwise have known. Again, without hammering the religious angle, you can write a skilful and relevant piece on, say, new pilgrims on old pilgrimage routes, dishes which began as ritual meals, the relationship between unresolved anxiety and some physical disorders, how to make a christingle – and why.

The festivals of the church's year offer almost endless possibilities for writing for the secular market. For example, not many secular readers these days will know what 'Advent' means, but they will find out as they read with interest about the significance of the Advent calendar or the Advent candle, both of which are top sellers in high street stores. Christingle oranges, pancakes, chocolate eggs and simnel cake are other easy 'link' items that will allow you to write up something of the religious angle. Candles and light generally, salt, oil – all are religious symbols which can be explained for a secular readership.

Remember, too, that our Christian culture has also left us a legacy of wonderful people to write about. You can find the traditional saints of old well documented in the *Oxford Dictionary of Saints* published by Clarendon Press. But don't necessarily go for the well-known favourites. Someone like St Bridget – who was reputed to have miraculously turned her bath water into beer for the benefit of visiting clergymen – will certainly make saleable copy for a secular outlet! And the more recent 'saints' such as Newton, Wilberforce, Shaftesbury, Livingstone, Josephine Butler, Mary Slessor, Gladys Aylward *et al* make for interesting reading, in either topic-related or anniversary slots.

UK secular personal-experience slots

Perhaps the most surprising development in secular magazines in recent years has been the shift, in some of the best-selling women's weeklies, to readers' own personal-experience articles in place of the more traditional features about famous people. You will find these personal stories in regular slots with titles such as *Reader Confidential, My True Love Story, Your Own Page, Real Life Drama, It Happened To Me, Personal Story* and *Behind Closed Doors*.

There are two reasons why these slots should be of interest to the religious writer. First of all, you will see that many of them are 'as told to' articles. This means that the piece as published, while written in the first person as if straight from the pen of the person whose story it is, has in fact been written by someone else assigned to do so by the magazine. Many of these stories deal with times of crisis and difficulty, and a writer who is also a Christian could be expected to bring an added dimension of care and sensitivity to the task of interviewing the subject.

If you would like to try this kind of writing and you are not already known to the features editor of your targeted magazine, the accepted approach is to 'trawl' your local and regional press for two or three stories which might lend themselves to national coverage in the style of your chosen magazine. You then send the cuttings to the features editor, with a sample of your own published work and a covering letter offering to write up the stories for the targeted slot. Or you could telephone first to sound out the editor about the stories you have in mind.

The other reason why these 'personal experience' slots should be of interest to the religious writer is that they provide a golden opportunity to get *your own* story into a secular magazine, along with its message of encouragement for others. Because it is a secular magazine, you will not, of course, pepper the piece with Bible verses or references to God. What you can do, though, is speak about faith and prayer and about circumstances being changed by a power outside of yourself, all of which have some meaning even for non-religious readers. Pieces like this have long been popular with the American markets, secular and religious. They are known as 'inspirational articles'.

The inspirational article

During an 'Open Forum' at a writers' conference I attended, one of the questions was: 'Is there a market in the UK for inspirational writing?' The answers from the experts and the comments from the floor added up to a certain amount of confusion – not about the potential market, but about the nature of the genre. Just what is 'inspirational writing'?

Obviously, it is writing that inspires, but there is more to it than that. Leaving religion aside for a moment, we can say that inspirational writing is based on the concept of 'negative' against 'positive'. The writer describes a situation producing negative emotions and/or consequences, which are satisfactorily resolved by the application of some positive abstract such as honesty, perseverance, coverage, or resilience. The outcome inspires the reader to believe that if he were in similar circumstances, he could apply the same 'positive' and achieve the same satisfactory result.

By this definition, inspirational writing does not have to be in any sense 'religious' writing. Much of the 'How I Coped . . .' kind of material in the reader-slots of today's secular magazines could be described as inspirational.

Within the religious market, of course, inspirational articles and books hinge on the fact that the 'positive' influence responsible for the resolution has something to do with God. Things are changed because of faith or prayer or divine intervention. And there are inspirational books and articles which fall somewhere in the middle – the change is brought about by the power of positive thinking, a new awareness of love or innocence or nature, some unseen unexplained force, or just fate.

Choose the best market

If you are thinking of writing up some of your own experiences as inspirational articles, think carefully about where to sell them. If you sell a story to a religious publisher, it will inspire its (presumably) religious readers, but in many ways you would be preaching to the converted. Would your story have even greater impact if it appeared in a secular publication? With subtlety and sensitivity you could still make sure that the reader knew what brought about the change.

Use the best style

When you are writing your inspirational article, don't *tell* the reader what happened in reported action. For example, 'Harry was very resentful about going to live in the nursing home' tells us the facts, but does not let us actually 'see' Harry or his feelings or the nursing home. The story comes to life for the reader when you *show* what happened, using the fiction techniques of characterisation and dialogue. Compare the bald statement about Harry with this little scene: 'Harry grunted at me as I entered his room. "Oh, it's you," he said, with a sniff. "Well, come in if you must, but mind where you walk. There's no room to swing a cat in this pokey hole." '

You also have to be careful not to get on your Sunday soapbox, even if you are writing for a religious market. Let the drama of the story speak for itself. You don't need to intrude with the 'author's voice' pointing out the theological implications of what is happening. Some religious publications will expect your story to portray some Biblical truth, and indeed some of the best inspirational stories hinge on that point where a Bible verse turned the main character in a different direction. But only mention a Bible reference if it is absolutely integral to the story as it happened.

Remember your reader

Don't use your inspirational article to remodel yourself into the better person you wish you were. Your reader will be expecting at least two things from your inspirational story. First, he wants to be involved, to identify with what is being described, so that he can begin to imagine your solution becoming his solution. So you will need to use recognisable situations (e.g. parents and teenage rebellion) and honest emotions (e.g. anger and/or despair in coping with teenage rebellion). If you shouted and threatened (or worse) long before you remembered to pray, then don't imply that your first response was rational and/or spiritual. This will not help a reader who is feeling inadequate.

Your reader also wants a solution, so he will be looking for what brought about your solution. If you are writing for a religious publication, your reader will want his personal faith to be strengthened by being drawn into the way you felt God's presence, or perhaps by an account of a moving conversion experience.

Explore all the options

There is not one kind of article which can be labelled 'the inspirational article'. The genre covers many categories, including the following:

Personal Experience
Not just dramatic incidents, but situations where you had to make a difficult decision, or you had to sort out your priorities.

Recovery After Illness/Accident
Give enough medical information to set the scene, but not every last detail – the reader wants to read a story about a person, not a medical case history. Be honest – give credit to doctors, not just to praying friends.

Coping with Illness/Disability
Explore the emotional problems of acceptance as well as the practical problems. Give details of support groups.

Self-Help for Personal or Behaviour Problems
'I've been there' testimonies, not just concerning drugs or alcohol, but such psychological problems as agoraphobia, loneliness, bereavement. Avoid the temptation to overdo the negative, or your piece will be unbalanced and uninspiring.

Relationships
The story of a healed relationship will strike a chord with most readers. You must show the problem that caused the deterioration, the circumstances that brought about recognition of the problem, as well as the actual reconciliation.

Nostalgia
Some specific past incident or person which left an indelible mark for good or ill on your life.

Adventure
An account of a person in a dangerous situation where faith and or prayer at a time of panic brought calm and peace.

How-To
Advice on specific action aimed at achieving a specific result, often in the format 'Ten Steps To . . .'

Conversion
A moving account of a religious encounter showing the 'before' and 'after', usually with lots of emotional impact for the reader.

More Abundant Living
The one kind of inspirational piece which is more about a topic than a person. Explore the benefits of some life-enhancing activity or attitude, such as laughter, tears, listening, leisure time, using (where appropriate) Bible verses, anecdotes, poems in such a way that the reader is inspired to introduce the same attitude or activity into his own life.

Famous People
Usually not an option unless you are a known writer and are commissioned to do an interview for a magazine. Readers are helped by an account of how someone they admire met with a particular problem and overcame it.

Personality Profile (not necessarily famous)
The achievements of some outstanding person within a particular field, told in a way that helps the reader apply the same 'positive' to his own situation.

Organisation or Charity
Not a potted history, but a picture of the work of the society revealed through a piece about a particular person, perhaps the founder, a present-day worker or someone who has been helped by the organisation.

Whatever kind of inspirational writing you undertake, it will stand more chance of being published if it is written simply, in a way that makes readers feel they are sharing the experience with you; if it is written with open honesty about the 'negative'; if it is written to read like fiction using dramatisation and dialogue; and if it is written in a way that shows the reader how to plug into the power that changed the 'negative' into 'positive'. Get it right, and there are countless markets awaiting you on both sides of the Atlantic.

15

WRITING AS PART OF A TEAM

A lonely business?

Yes, writing is a solitary pursuit. But if what you write is intended for publication, then your lonely hours at the keyboard are in fact the first link in the chain between your original inspiration and the thoughts that are generated in the readers' minds as they read your words in print. Think of your work in print, and you are immediately part of a team, along with the editors, sub-editors, typesetters, printers, publishers, distributors and retailers who form the chain that passes your inspired words to the reader.

The newspaper/magazine chain

When the manuscript of your magazine or newspaper article arrives in the post (or your electronic copy arrives at the computer if you are *very* hi-tech!) it is read by the appropriate editor. If it is what they want, you will be notified and offered the appropriate fee, and your piece will be stored away ready for use.

Some newspaper and magazine editors have a grid plan - sometimes fixed to a wall where it is always visible and accessible - with the publication dates of future issues written across the top and the regular slots listed down the side. As material is accepted and stored, a note is made in the appropriate square, so editors can tell at a glance where new material is still required. Many an excellent article is rejected simply because the appropriate squares are all filled, and that's just unfortunate. Of course, an article might be rejected because there is no slot on the grid for material of that kind or of that length, and that's inexcusable – the writer didn't study the targeted market.

When it is time to process all the accepted material for a particular issue, a sub-editor arranges your stored material to suit the house style, slotting in sub-headings and sidebars where relevant. Photographs and advertisements are processed separately to fit spaces left for them.

The completed pages are then sent to the typesetter and printers. All the printed pages are then collated and folded to make up the magazine or paper.

Bundles of finished magazines are sent by rail and road to the various wholesalers and/or retailers, in time for the shops to have them on the shelves on publication day. Many religious magazines make a further journey, from the Christian bookshop to the church bookstall.

The book chain

There is nothing to stop anyone writing a book and then taking the manuscript to a printer, and paying to have it printed and the copies bound in book form. Indeed, this 'self-publishing' method is widely used these days, especially as many small printers now have desktop publishing computers and litho printing machines which make typesetting and page layout easy, and small print-runs viable.

Self-publishing, where the author pays the printer and takes responsibility for selling all the books, is a respectable option, particularly for well-written books which have a specialised and limited market, such as church histories and small anthologies. But self-publishing is not to be confused with vanity publishing, which is dealt with later in this chapter.

If you are writing a book for a wider market, then you will need an established publisher to process it and get it to its targeted reader.

The publisher's commissioning editor selects a suitable book from the many manuscripts sent to a publisher, or finds the best writer for a proposed book. It is usually the commissioning editor who keeps in touch with the author while the book is being written.

Rather than approach a publisher direct, some writers send their manuscripts to a literary agent, who undertakes to find a publisher for it, for a percentage of the book's earnings. As the agent usually negotiates a higher percentage of sales for the author, this should not cost the writer anything. However, in order to make a living, literary agents need to concentrate on successful writers, and they are often unwilling to take on an unpublished writer. Agents and their special interest areas are listed in the *Writers' and Artists' Yearbook* and *The Writer's Handbook*.

The publisher's copy editor (or desk editor, or production editor) checks the completed manuscript, corrects spelling mistakes and other minor errors, queries ambiguities, and generally does what is necessary to tidy up the completed manuscript and put it into a format which is interpreted into book pages by the typesetter and printer.

The edited manuscript then goes to the typesetter, and from there to the printer – sometimes to more than one printer if, for example, there are colour illustrations. The book's pages are printed on huge sheets of paper which then have to be guillotined and correctly collated, folded and bound. The number of pages in a book is usually a multiple of sixteen pages, but adjustments can be made in the book's length by the use of a larger or smaller typeface. When the books are printed and bound, they are delivered to the publisher.

Booksellers find out about new books from publishers' catalogues, but some publishers and distributors (see below) also employ sales representatives, 'reps', who travel around the country visiting booksellers, informing them which books are currently available and what they are like, and also bringing advance notice of books which are going to be published soon. The rep then passes orders from the bookseller back to the publisher or distributor.

Some religious publishers organise their own distribution of books, but others use a professional distributor. Distributors are, in effect, wholesalers who keep bulk supplies of titles from many publishers in huge warehouses. This system allows the bookseller to order books by several different publishers all from the same distributor, which makes for a fast and flexible service to get *your* book on to his shelves where the purchaser can see it.

The purchaser may be a book agent who buys religious books on a 'sale or return' basis for the local church bookstall.

Eventually, after every member of the team has played their part, a new book is opened by a new reader and someone – at last – reads the words *you* were inspired to write, in those solitary moments at the other end of the chain.

Vanity publishing

Vanity publishing is a way of making money out of people's desire to see themselves in print.

This is how it works. A vanity publisher advertises for authors' manuscripts. The author is asked to pay a large sum to the publisher (always larger than the cost of printing), and in return they take delivery of several thousand books which they then have to sell. The vanity publisher may promise to promote the book in literary journals, but he will ask the author to pay for any advertising. The vanity publisher will not be interested in actually marketing the book, sending reps round the booksellers getting orders, because he's already had his money. He won't be supplying the usual distributors. With vanity publishing, the author is the distributor.

Just think about that for a moment. Imagine your garage full of books, then do a rough count of all your friends and relations. Subtract – and you are left with a garage not quite full of books. It can be worse. I have heard of disappointed authors who have even taken delivery of *unbound* books, or only the first batch of books, after which no more have ever arrived. (At least they can get their car in the garage, but that's small comfort.)

Perhaps you think I exaggerate. You have quite a good relationship with the booksellers in your town and you are pretty confident they will sell your book for you. I've no doubt they will if it is *self*-published and of local interest. But reputable booksellers will rarely handle books from vanity publishers.

Apart from any moral considerations, they risk their reputation by selling a shoddy product. The vanity publisher will have assured the author that their book is brilliant, whether it is or it isn't, because he wants the author's money. So a book from a vanity publisher may *look* good (sometimes they do), but the contents may be appalling.

How do you know if you are dealing with a vanity publisher? That's easy. With *very* rare exceptions (for example, limited market poetry anthologies), a reputable publisher will never ask an author to finance the production of a book or to purchase copies.

There are three enormous advantages in finding a reputable publisher to process your manuscript in the traditional way. The first is that the publisher supplies all the up-front money, including an 'advance' to the author, based on the agreed percentage of the expected number of sales. The second is that the publisher's editorial staff can advise the author and revise the manuscript so that the published work is as good as it can possibly be. It is in the publisher's interest to make it good so that it sells and he gets his money back. And the third advantage? If a reputable publisher thinks your book is worth publishing, then you *know* it is good!

Meeting other writers

Even though the writing process is a solitary pursuit, a writer need never feel totally isolated. There is a network of writers' circles across the UK, most of which are listed in Jill Dick's *Directory of Writers' Circles* (available from Jill Dick, Oldacre, Horderns Park Road, Chapel-en-le-Frith, Derbyshire, SK12 6SY). Your local library should have details of any local writers' groups and your Adult Education Office will have details of classes. Further local information should also be available from your local Arts Association.

There are two major annual residential gatherings for writers: the *Caerleon Writers' Holiday* (details from D.L. Anne Hobbs, 30 Pant Road, Newport, Gwent, NP9 5PR) and *Writers' Summer School* at Swanwick (details from Philippa Boland, The Red House, Mardens Hill, Crowborough, Sussex, TN6 1XN).

If you would value the encouragement of fellow Christians as you write, there are regional and national events organised by the *Fellowship of Christian Writers* (details from the Membership Secretary, 3 Over Close, Paignton, South Devon, TQ3 3PX) and *Christian Writers' Forum* (27 Old Gloucester Street, London, WC1N 3XX).

When you consider all the people you are working with in the publishing chain, and all the other religious writers (and others) waiting for you to bounce your ideas off them, you have to admit that writing is perhaps not such a lonely business after all!

149